HIGHER ART

A Discipline to Kindle Life

Vasant Avarsekar

Popular Prakashan
www.popularprakashan.com

Published by Harsha Bhatkal
for Popular Prakashan Pvt. Ltd.
301, Mahalaxmi Chambers
22, Bhulabhai Desai Road
Mumbai 400026
www.popularprakashan.com

First Published 2014

(4383)
ISBN 978-81-7991-824-1

Design: Mahendra Ghanekar

Printed by
Saurabh Printers Pvt. Ltd.
B-280, Okhla Industrial Area
Phase 1, New Delhi-110 020

FOREWORD

At an exhibition in 1989, in the premises of Sir J.J. School of Art, Mumbai, renowned contemporary artist Laxman Shrestha was seen intensely engrossed in admiring Professor Vasant Avarsekar's canvases. He then sought out the senior artist, and enquired with candid wonderment, "How is it that I did not know you earlier?"

One can understand why Professor Avarsekar was not discovered earlier by someone like Laxman Shrestha. It was because he was busy serving the cause of art through a different line of destiny. One may say, lecturing on Art History and Aesthetics took away precious decades from the productive years of Avarsekar as a practicing fine artist. But then that's how I, among thousands of other art students, had the privilege to know him in our formative years, much earlier than 1989.

Many art stalwarts over centuries have also acquired the status of great teachers. But in most cases, their pupils were apprentices learning the craft in their studios, sometimes merely imitating the masters and supplementing their productive efforts. Avarsekar taught the essence of art to a large number of students year after year across diverse disciplines, expanding their minds and sensibilities, empowering the talented ones to realise their true potential as original artists.

At J.J., then considered as Asia's premier art institute, there were many teachers who pursued a diverse and active life as creative artists, beyond their lecturing hours. Avarsekar, since he taught theory, and taught really well, stood apart from that kind of aura. His experiments with creation of art remained private and confined to a relatively limited number of paintings that he produced during his peak period as a professor. Finally, his retirement from academia in 1989 ushered him deep into the sanctum of productive creativity, where his rare personal qualities combining retrospection and introspection, sensibility and skill, theory and practice, found joyous and prolific expression.

Intense love of life and art, and the joy of interface with students had kept him young in mind and body, and there was no dearth of physical and creative energy, as Avarsekar took giant leaps as a sensitive and insightful painter, bringing into the picture his deep and expansive understanding of the universal philosophy and psychology of artistic endeavour.

Discussing art and creating art do not always overlap happily, but when they do, one can expect a rich harvest. This book, since its conception, has had that in its favour. Relaxed and comfortable under his own scholastic shadow, Avarsekar the artist has illustrated this book with his own paintings. Paintings, where every brush stroke is guided by intuitive yet deliberate application of form, colour and composition. His artistic persona is comprehensive and masterly, where the seeker confronting his paintings can find cause, meaning and sophistication in all the elemental choices made, be it of depth of concept and sensibility, or diversity of technique and skill.

Avarsekar's evaluation of true art does not stoop to make politically correct noises. He is candid and honest in airing his views without fear or favour. Much of his observation in this book should lead to the infusion of fresh oxygen in the polluted arena of commercial or populist aspects of the contemporary art scene.

In the same breath, of course, the scope of his discussion of art transcends time and territory. After a sweeping glimpse of the objective grandeur and psychosomatic upheavals of Western art movements, he returns as a pilgrim of nobility to Indian art, and in juxtaposition of the two, time and again, he paints a panoramic canvas of expansive vision. A vision that hints at something he considers the ultimate promise of art: Unity with Nature, in both the micro and macro dimensions.

Like his favourite subject of trees, Avarsekar's artistic persona remains rooted and revelled in Nature. The beauty and utility of a tree are both symbol and subject of much of his artistic expression. The artist and the humanist in him were awakened early in life in his dalliance and dialogue with Nature, amid the pristine scenic beauty of his birthplace. Today, in his twilight years, the artist and the humanist still smile and sing together in his thoughts and paintings.

It is fortunate that as both teacher and artist, Professor Avarsekar has been in a unique position to gift this book to the art lovers of the world. Sensitive minds that glide through these illuminating pages might well ask, "How is it that such a book was not written earlier...?"

— **Ashok Roy**
Mumbai, 2013

PREFACE

I believe that all individuals are, to some extent, artists and that all artists are, from first to the last, a united human race in activities related to creation and enjoyment of art. However, successful artists are those who bring in excess of time and talent to create unique art works of outstanding beauty and quality. The sacred purpose of art needs to be, as far as possible, to convey a complete human experience of the world. The fine arts recognise the vital forces within us to create and give to the world enduring forms of art for the sake of exploration and development of humanity in its totality. The secret of art is, therefore, neither to exist for its own sake nor to embellish life and invent forms of pleasure and fashions, but to present to the world a total human experience of the spirit of the time, place and society.

Art is also an autonomous activity influenced by the material and spiritual conditions of our existence. Visual art expressed in visual language has its own reality and purpose. It is also a mode of knowledge. It contributes to the process of integration of culture and civilisation. The fine art of painting, sculpture and architecture has necessary relations with politics and religion. The creative artists and art patrons are, therefore, responsible for a progressive human destiny.

The modern world of science and technology differs from the past as a result of industrial revolutions. A new age of machines has replaced the earlier traditional cultures. In the 20th century after the two World Wars, the conditions of life and living have changed with such a speed that the people have changed and are changing. Inventions like the movie cameras and computers have brought the visual world closer, giving a new trend to the world of art. The characteristic temper of our age is a mixture of restlessness, obsession for progress, comforts and novelty. Artists of the 20th century also responded to the change of environments and were successful in breaking the traditional art forms and art ideas. New concepts of art styles and techniques, under different names or 'isms' by different groups of artists, poets and philosophers came into vogue. Cubism, a style of experimental art of Picasso and Braque was iconoclastic because it completely destroyed the grace and beauty of traditional human figures and natural objects. This of course shatters the old ideas of compositions and perspective. But Cubism and its derivatives were accepted then because the concept of reality was separated from that of appearance and resemblance of nature's form. The ordinary vision was no longer considered important. Moreover, artists were free to conceive forms and symbols experimentally without reference to nature. The resultant art was classified as Abstract Art.

Scientists with their knowledge and experiments create abstract forces and use them for convenience and comforts of mankind with modern technology, and machines. The basic motivation of scientific discoveries is the human intelligence and not the emotional forces of sympathy and love which motivate the art creations. In the modern world, science is used both for creative and destructive purposes and the people of the world are in constant fear and anxiety. I think that the rapid obsolescence of ideas and things gives to life a tentative and temporary quality and makes confusion a constant in its ever changing patterns. This is also true about the 20th century art of the world.

My retrospect is a glimpse of 20th century Modern Art and Indian traditional art. I have tried to stress the importance and necessity of art ideas, philosophy, psychology and aesthetic sense in practice and appreciation of visual arts. Art discipline demands skilful practice by talented individuals of knowledge and intuition. I am convinced that one of the secrets of creation is the mystery of vibrations and rhythms, their influence, method and mode of working consciousness. The whole world is the play and display of consciousness, the cause and effect of existence.

Since art is a process of creation by the artists, I think introspection or looking within is very essential for growth and evolution of the artist's own personality. Part-II of this book deals with my introspection which reflects my personal thinking and experience of paintings I have been creating and exhibiting. I have included perceptual and emotional contents of my childhood experience because I feel they have much to do with my concepts and philosophy of art.

— Vasant Avarsekar

Mumbai, 2014

CONTENTS

PART I

RETROSPECTION

MY PAINTINGS: ABSTRACT, REAL AND CONCEPTUAL

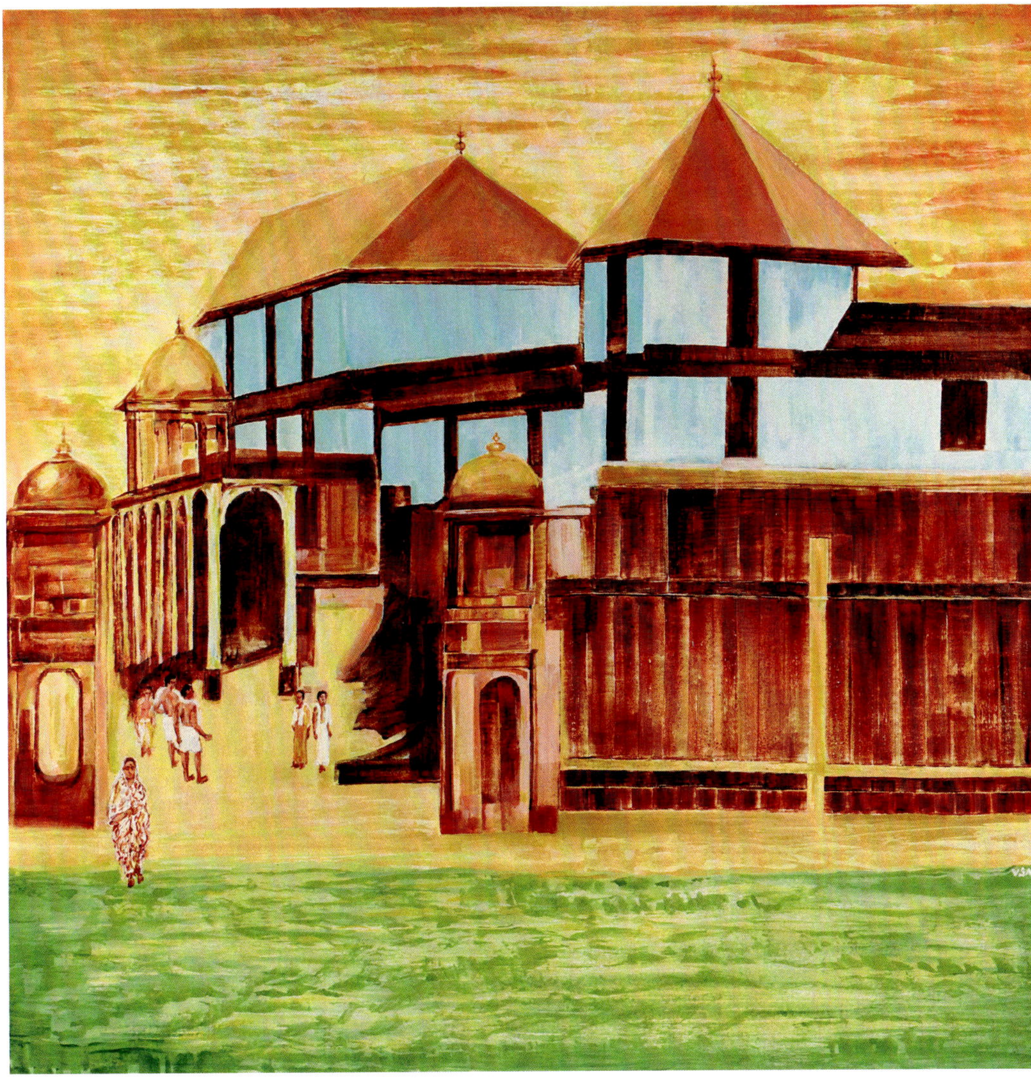

Temple-Dharmasthal

36”x36” • Acrylic on Canvas

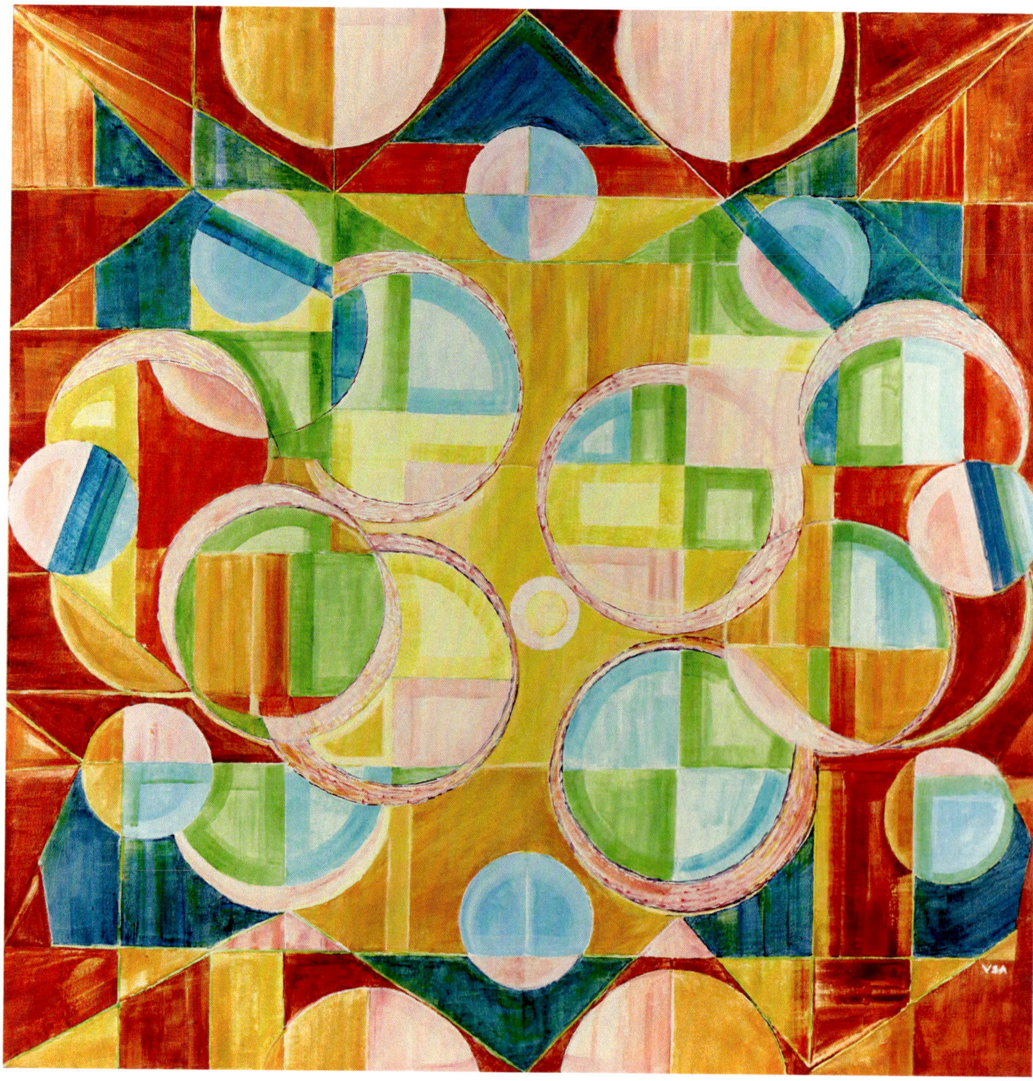

Circular Composition

36"x36" • Acrylic on Canvas

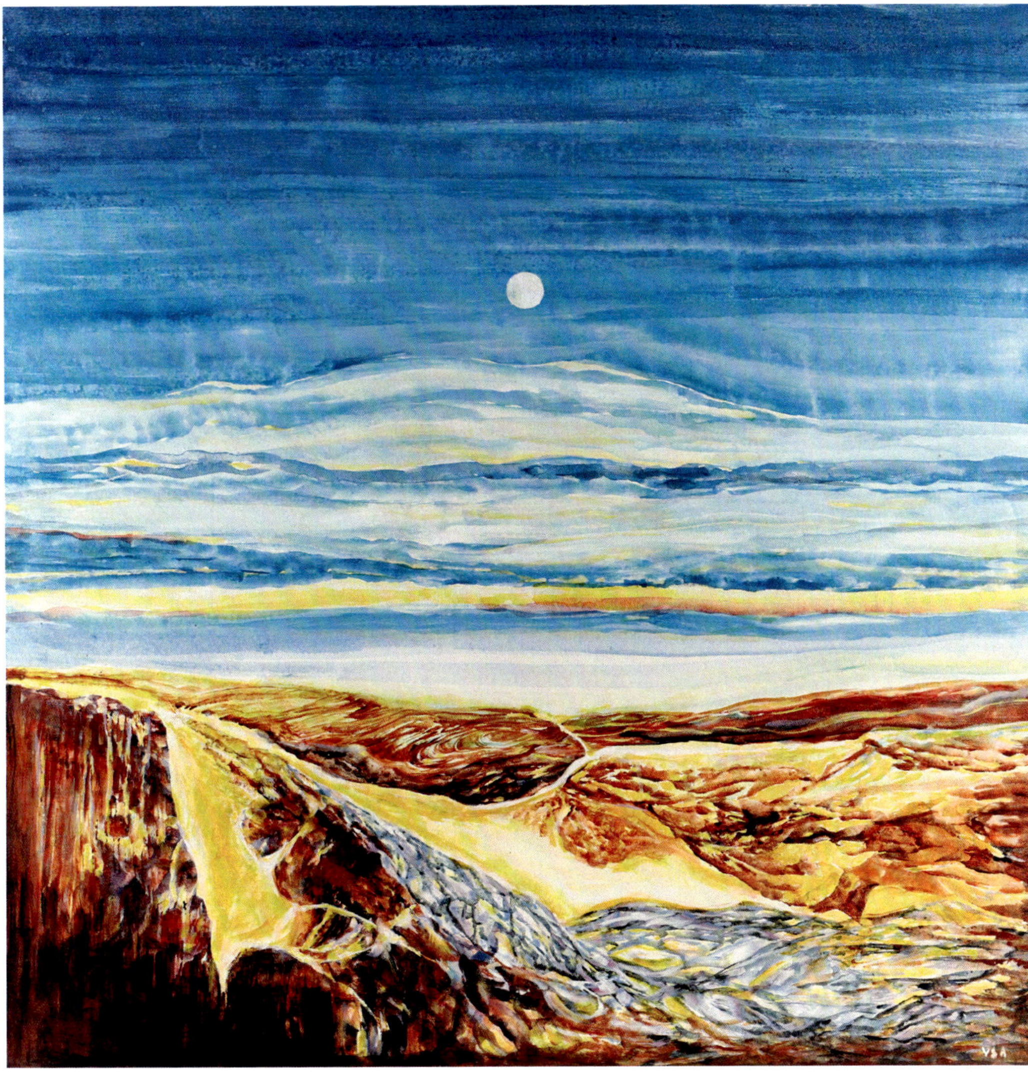

Moonlight Landscape

36"x36" • Acrylic on Canvas

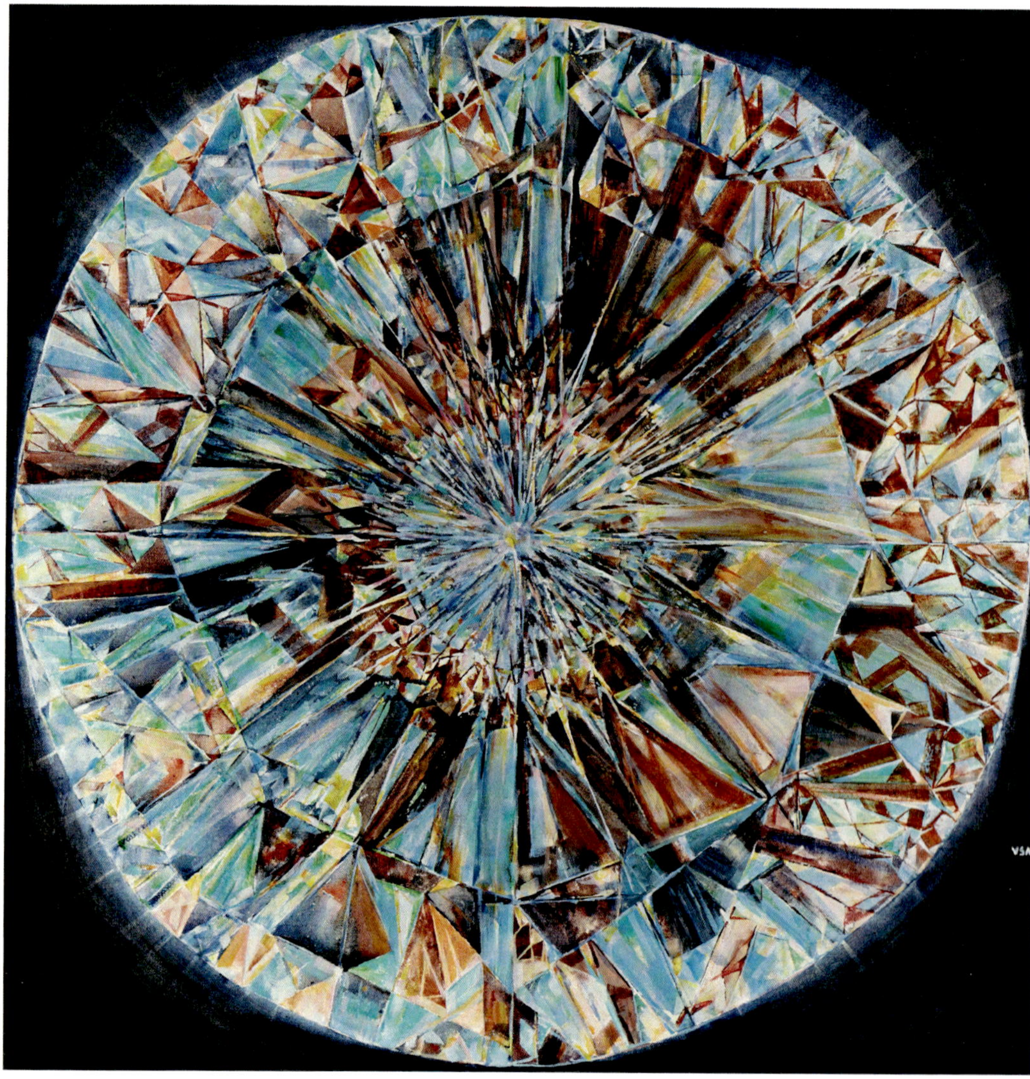

Colour Refractions

32"x32" • Acrylic on Canvas

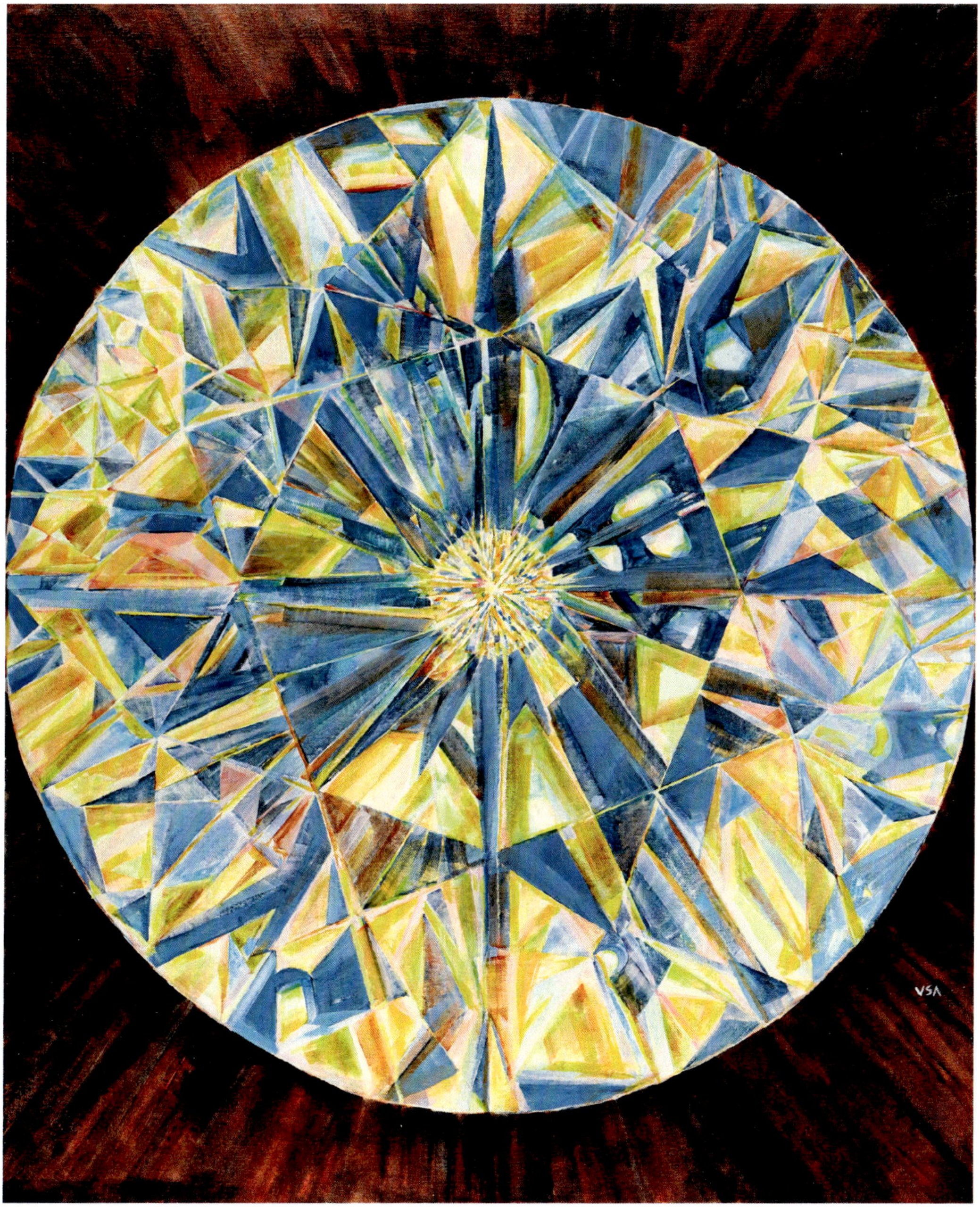

Colour Refractions

32”x36” • Acrylic on Canvas

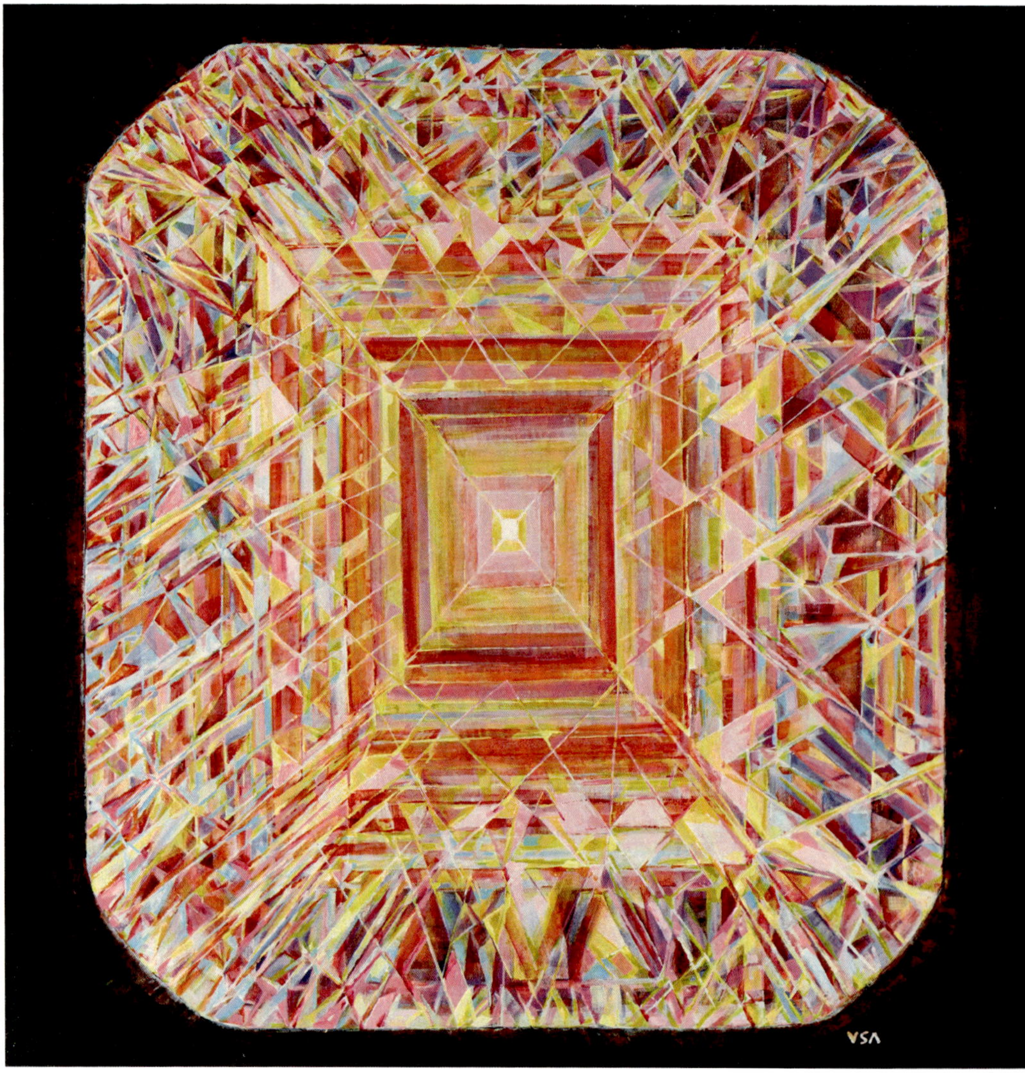

Colour Refractions

32"x32" • Acrylic on Canvas

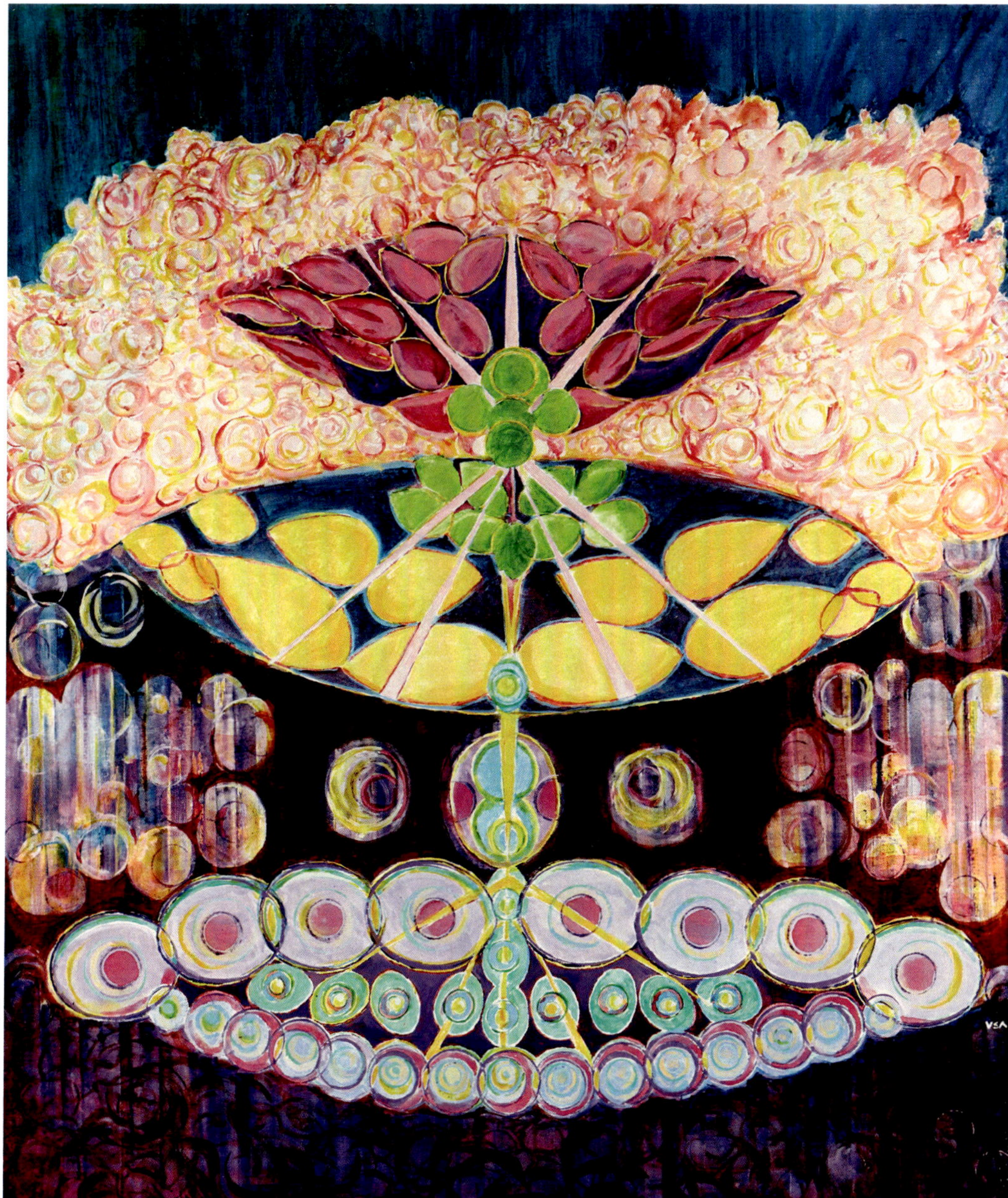

Polarisation and Evolution

36”x40” • Acrylic on Canvas

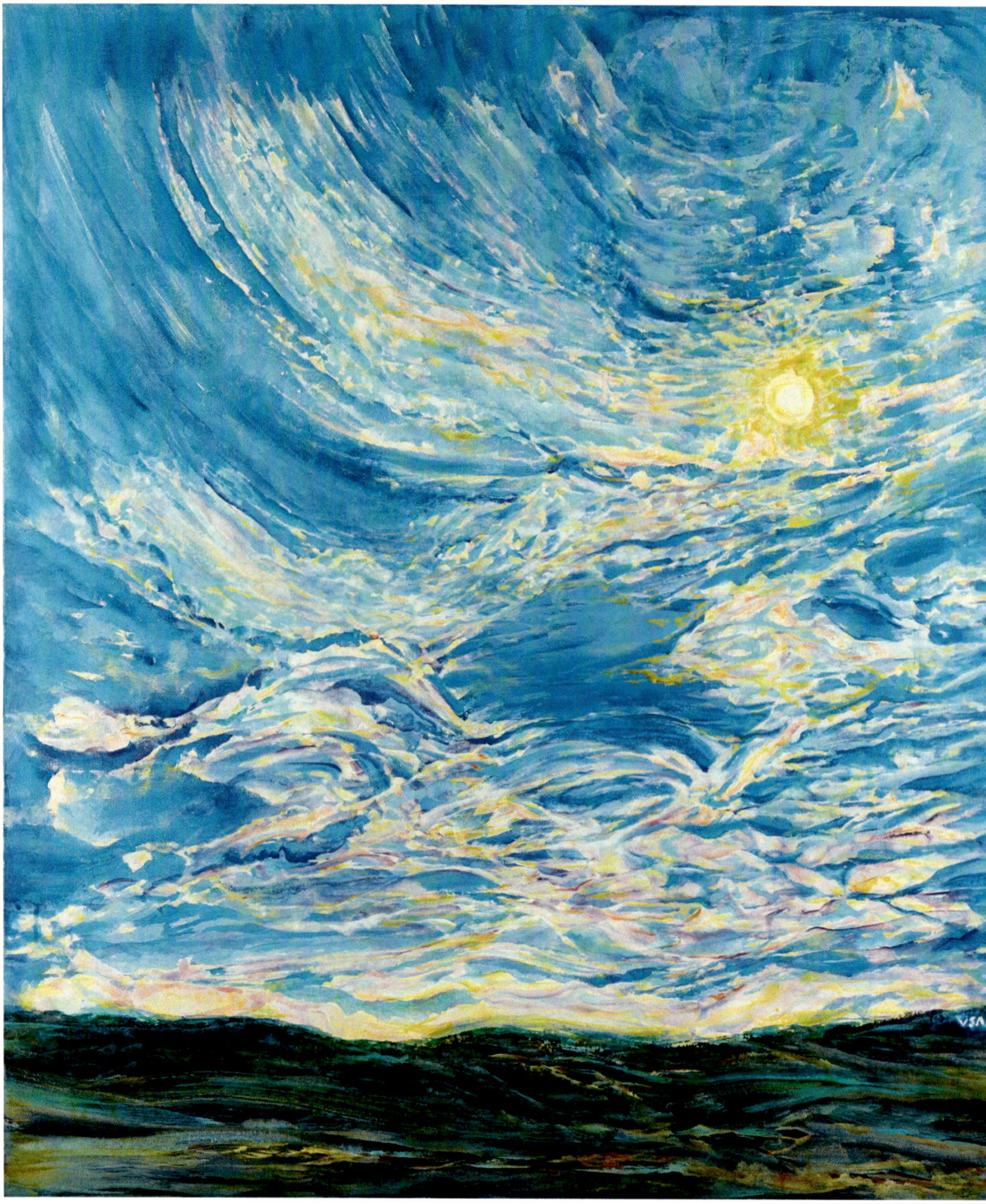

Skyscape

36"x42" • Acrylic on Canvas

Nature and Origin of Fine Art

The understanding and appreciation of creative art is closely related to the development of the human mind and culture. The work of art, visible and tangible, is a kind of persisting event that needs discerning appreciation for its enjoyment. Moral and religious ideas of mankind were all-powerful in ancient past and their art works have the capacity of arousing our present interest. Certain creations of past and present continue to give us unique joy irrespective of our awareness of who, when and where those beautiful works were created. These achievements seem to be due to sincere and dedicated attempts of individuals to exploit the ideas and technology of their times to the full extent. But the most surprising features of these art works are that those creative artists have succeeded in achieving a total harmony in their works with aesthetic consciousness. Creation of fine art works, as in noble literature, constitutes what is valued for its own sake in the ambience of our present life. But let us not forget that the central matter to be elucidated in fine art is the value of beauty for human life, implied both in practice and recognition.

The word ART has come from Latin 'ARS' meaning skill. The question has been asked, "What is Art?" The discussions have introduced elements of conscious purpose into the realm of our personality, where both our faculties of creation and enjoyment have been spontaneous and semi-conscious.

Philosophers, art critics and aestheticians aim at supplying us very definite standards by which to guide our judgement of art productions. We have heard judges in modern time giving verdicts according to some special rules of their own making for the dethronement of immortals whose supremacy was unchallenged for centuries.

The world of science which is the world of abstract force, is not the world of reality to the artist's personality. There is another world which is real to him. He sees it, feels it, and he deals with it with all his emotions. Its endless mystery cannot be analysed or measured. The world of art has an intimate relationship with his visual world. Art, like life itself, has grown by its own impulse, and man has taken pleasure in it, without definitely knowing what it is. All true art has its origin in emotions and sentiments. Immortal works of art, of any civilised country, remain not only in monumental buildings and temple architecture, but in pictures and music and workmanship in stone and metal. The true principle of art is the principle of unity, and the analytical treatment will never discover the vital point in art.

What is it in man and artist, that asserts its immortality, in spite of the obvious fact of death? It is not his body or his mental organisation. It is that deeper unity, that ultimate mystery in him, which is in his mind, yet grows beyond his mind. And this consciousness of the infinite in the personal man, always strives to make its expressions immortal, and to make the whole world its own.

I believe that a true artist is in direct contact, through these expressions, with the Supreme Entity who reveals to him the world of endless beauty across the lightless world of facts.

Art is a gift of nature given only to mankind, to kindle life through creative activities on this planet.

The essential nature of art is to be found in the artist's personality and capacity to create a synthetic and self consistent world. It is not to be found in the world of dreams and fantasy, but a world of convincing representation of totality of individual experience, gained by higher perceptions of some aspects of universal truths. Art is therefore an autonomous activity influenced by material conditions of existence. As a mode of knowledge art is distinct and contributes to the process of integration of cultures and civilisations. For the people of aesthetic sensibility and higher perceptions, art is everywhere in its manifestations, universal and eternal. Significance of art to mankind is obvious as it has left its landmarks on every civilisation of historical past. Art is therefore a mode of knowledge, and the world of art is a system of knowledge for understanding and experiencing the environments surrounding life and living.

Although some contradictions and conflicts exist in understanding and defining art, we may accept in principle that creating and enjoying art is an experience of beauty, peace and harmony. This is also the essence of our spiritual existence as only human beings are gifted by nature for creative revelations.

Fundamental Principles of Fine Art

Beauty and Harmony

There is no single definition of 'Beauty' that can be said to have met with universal acceptance. Among the ancients, the fundamental theory of beauty was connected with the notions of rhythm, symmetry, harmony of parts, regularity and repose. Among the Moderns, we find that the idea of significance, expressiveness, and also conceptions of characteristics have been emphasised in defining beauty. Ancient Indians equated beauty with truth and the sublime, (satyam, shivam, sunderam). The recognition of these ancient and modern thoughts as the constituent elements for the definition of beauty needs to be accepted for understanding and appreciation of the fine art of the 21st century.

In my 25 years of teaching subjects like art history, aesthetics and their applicability in conceiving art ideas for creative process by higher art students, I have come across more than 25 definitions of beauty and the beautiful, by eminent artists, philosophers and psychologists. The very fact that so many different definitions of beauty are in existence we may conclude that the 'beauty and beautiful' are abstract and real with many dimensions including the mystical and metaphysical. The word beauty is inclusive of the concept of hierarchy. It is therefore imperative that the people concerned with constructive criticism, appreciations and selections of significant visual art of extreme beauty should make themselves familiar with certain terms and their clear meanings related to the description of art works, and the process of creation of such works. In addition to verbal knowledge, a good judge of art needs a sensitive mind with a mature sensibility and a critical 'eye' for choosing the best of art work from the rest of illusionary works. He also needs to have a conviction that the fundamental principle of fine art is beauty and truth. A beautiful work of art has a beautiful soul which resonates with our aesthetic consciousness.

Renowned modern scientist Albert Einstein said, "The most beautiful and the most profound emotion we can experience is the sensation of the mystical. It is the source of all true art and science". Where there is beauty there is mystery and truth.

Nature and Art

We are not only the part of nature but nature ourselves — Tagore

It is generally agreed that all beauty is in perception and imagination i.e. Beauty lies in the eyes of the beholders. But the quantum of joy of the beautiful experienced in the presence of the landscape or any other reflective Abstract Art work inspired by nature or otherwise, varies with different individuals. This aspect of human experience cannot be explained with a statement like, different people have different tastes. It is so because firstly, the joy of the beautiful is limited for each percipient to the range of his own eyes and ears as exercised in the external world. Secondly, the insight and power of enjoyment to which the beauty of nature is relative, are required to be disciplined and intensified by aesthetic training and culture.

Beauty in nature does not exist in the form of recorded statements or communicable contents. It passes into the province of art not by sudden transition but by continuous modifications depending upon disciplined and intensified faculty of the artistic mind. A completed work of art is a definite thing born out of a creative spirit of the artistic mind, and may not even represent any natural object. Artists have extended the boundaries of natural beauty by their superior insights into the expressive capabilities of natural scenes and objects. Nature, therefore, is a province of beauty in which every human being is his own artist. The quantum of joy of the beauty experienced by both, the artist and art appreciator is not due to individual taste but definitely on account of their capability to interpret, understand and feel with a sensitive mind and aesthetic consciousness. Creativity of a mature artistic mind is the expression of realisation and revelation of truth within and without. Plastic art of painting and sculpture is not a mirror of common perception but an expression of something great and reasonable emerging from the heightened perception in sensuous form. A beautiful material thing is produced by participation in reason issuing from the divine. In that beautiful material the soul recognises an affinity to itself. This affinity consists in participation, in reason and form and is co-extensive with the beautiful. Colours show their own forms when applied on the canvas or paper by the artist with specific intentions.

The Supreme Being is giving himself through the world of nature and the artist in making it his own - like a painting which he realises by finding himself in it. Reality is the expression of personality - like a poem, like a work of art. If the artist's personality leaves the centre of his world then in a moment it loses all its attributes. The artist knows that the gift of his art is his personal, given to him by the Supreme Being. The process of receiving this gift can be classified and generalised by science, but not the gift itself, which is the soul unto the soul. Therefore, it can only be realised by the soul in joy, and not analysed by the reason of logic.

The Artist and his Observation

We all observe. But different persons observe the same object or objects with different degrees of curiosity and involvement. Intense observation is a starting point for a new vision enlightening one's mind.

Many people sit under trees and also observe the fruits falling from the trees when they are ripe. They simply pick them for eating. But it was Isaac Newton's questioning nature of the inquisitive mind which kept wondering why the fruits were not going up in the sky, was enlightened on the gravitational force of the earth. This discovery is not something new but an extension of his observant mind where it existed. The artist is part and parcel of nature with a gift; he can penetrate deeper into the world of beauty and nature with his intense observation and intuitive faculty of mind to seek the truth and beauty. Critical observation is required as a means to judge the right and wrong of an art work created for an exhibition.

The Artist and his Perception

In visual art the 'eye' and the light play a vital role in sensual perception. When the artist is not painting or creating any work of art, it does not mean that he ceases to be an artist. As a matter of fact his keen and intense observations and resultant perceptions grow with him during the interim periods. It may be said that art grows with the artist. Therefore it becomes a necessity for an artist to paint or be occupied with creative activities. In the course of time his mind becomes capable of transmitting feelings of higher perceptions with imagination and intuitive truth.

In the final analysis the artist's enlightened higher perceptions matched by acquired perfection of skill enables him to create distinct works of quality and character.

Modern scientists have growing scientific interest in psychology and the emergence of its new branch called parapsychology which enquires into the extraordinary faculties of the human mind. Extrasensory perceptions such as telepathy which were once considered elusive phenomena are being investigated to discover the natural abilities with an expanded field of human consciousness. The gift of an artist should enable him to evolve into the ethical and spiritual man in his pursuit of beauty in fine art.

Study of Subjects for Comprehension of Fine Art

In creating and appreciating Modern Secular Art, study of subjects like History of World Art, Aesthetics, Philosophy, Psychology and other related subjects contribute immensely in the development and understanding of the artist's art and ideas. But the vitality of art depends on the inborn faculty of the artist with nature's gift.

Aesthetics

It is a branch of philosophy that deals with questions of beauty, artistic tastes and merits. Artists involved in creative process are not directly concerned with aesthetic theories or discussions. It is said that aesthetics to the artists is like ornithology to the birds with nature's gift for flying. However, art critics and writers will be benefited with the study while offering verbal comments and opinions on the art works of different styles and character.

Aesthetic Consciousness

A sensitive mind can be disciplined and developed in many dimensions. Aesthetic consciousness relates to that aspect of consciousness of mind which seeks and penetrates into the world of beauty and beautiful things, both natural and man-made. Aesthetic joy is a unique experience of the joy of beauty and truth of unity in harmony. The science of aesthetics investigates the conditions in which things are regarded as beautiful; it can give no explanation of the origin of beauty.

Is Fine Art a Form of Meditation?

Meditation may be defined as a divine form of contemplation with a discipline and technique for achieving harmony and oneness.

Swamy Chinmayanand writes – "Our physical, mental, intellectual and spiritual personalities must be blended into one harmonious whole. Meditation is the technique for achieving this harmony. It is the highest spiritual discipline. Through meditation we experience peace within ourselves. Wars between desires end. Conflicts between duties no longer torment us. The mind is able to view life as a whole".

Meditation, as defined by Swami Chinmayanand, is the highest spiritual discipline to experience peace within ourselves. It is a holistic practice where all desires are controlled by the mind with complete realisation of the phenomena of the world. Such a practice can elevate the person to the highest spiritual state of 'stand still' mind (sthita prajnya) to receive the bliss of supra-consciousness. A spiritual discipline of meditation and contemplation demands not only observation and higher perception, but a regular practice of austerity and purity combined with unshakable faith and devotion of the highest order to be one with the supreme reality.

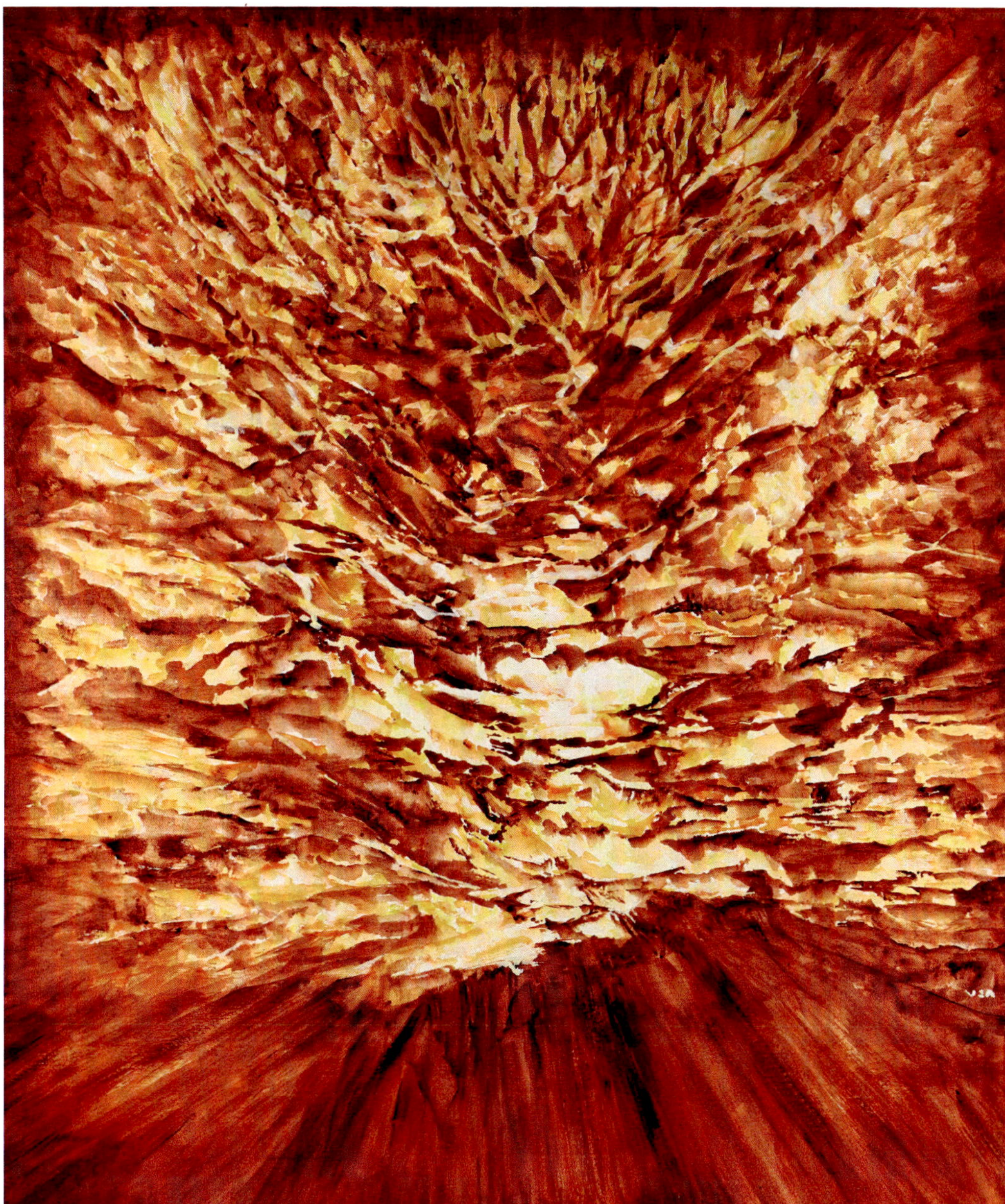

Dispel the Dark

36”x42” • Acrylic on Canvas

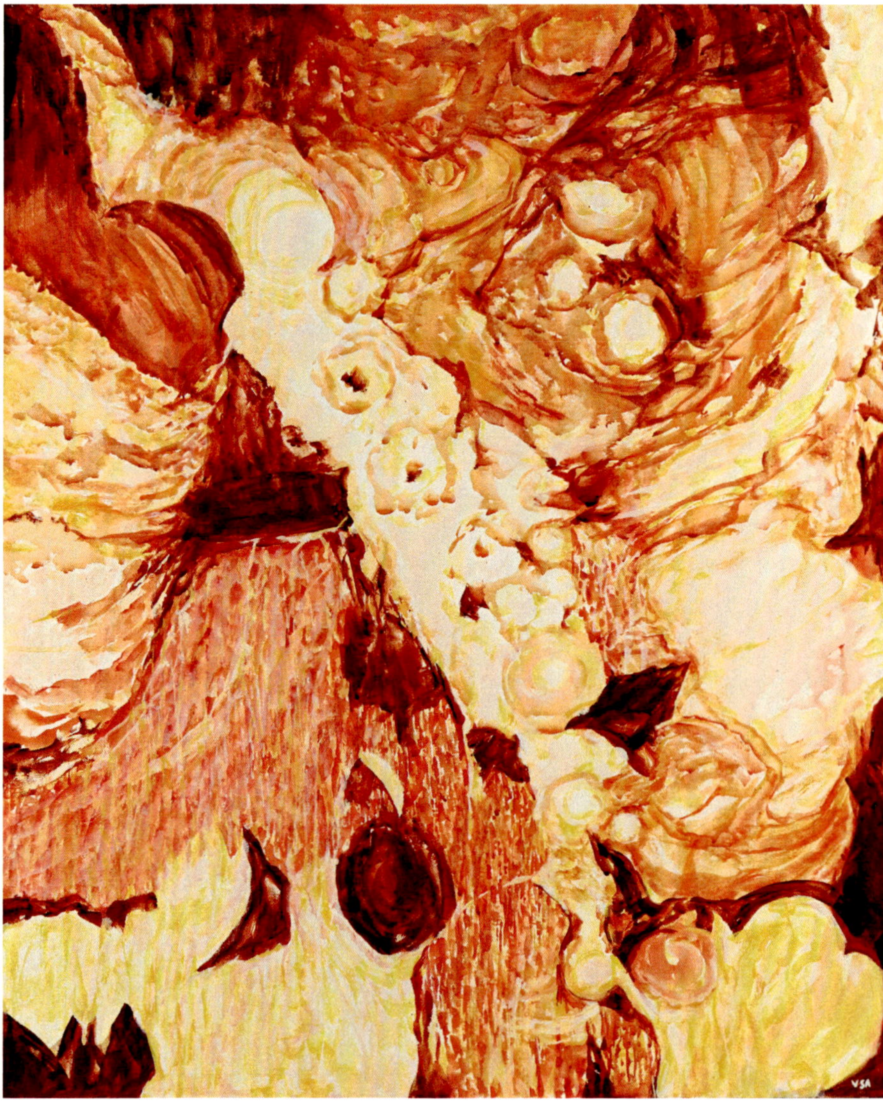

Blossoming

30”x40” • Acrylic on Canvas

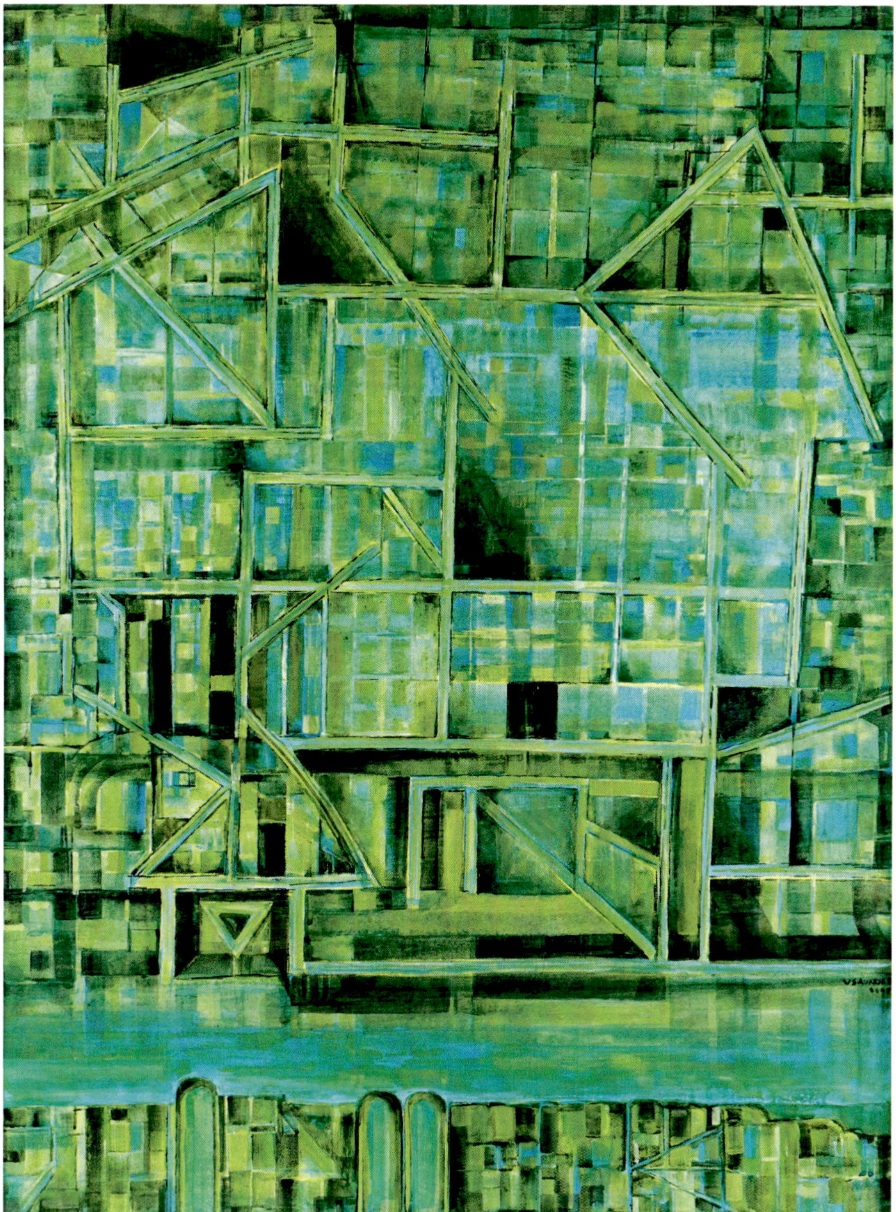

Geometry, Art and Aesthetics

30"x40" • Acrylic on Canvas

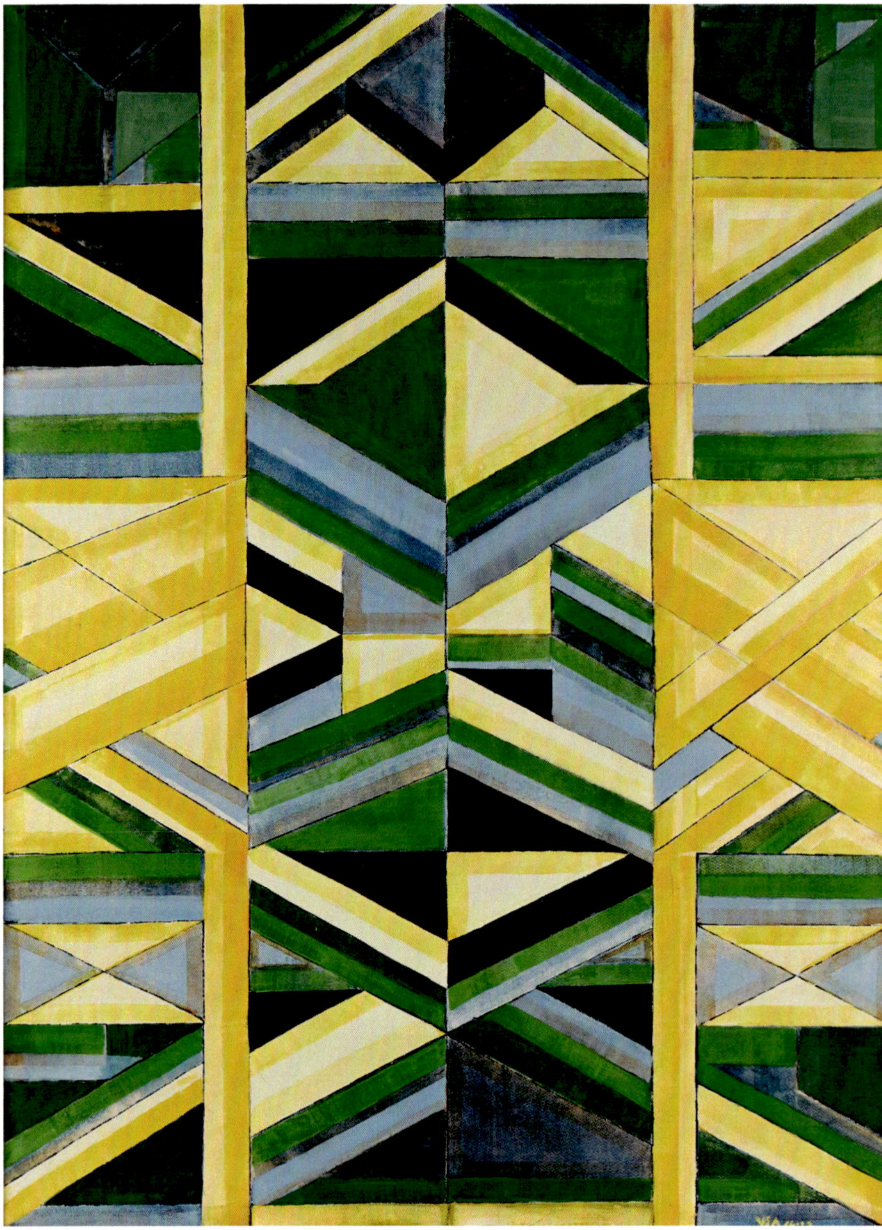

Geometry, Art and Aesthetics

30”x40” • Acrylic on Canvas

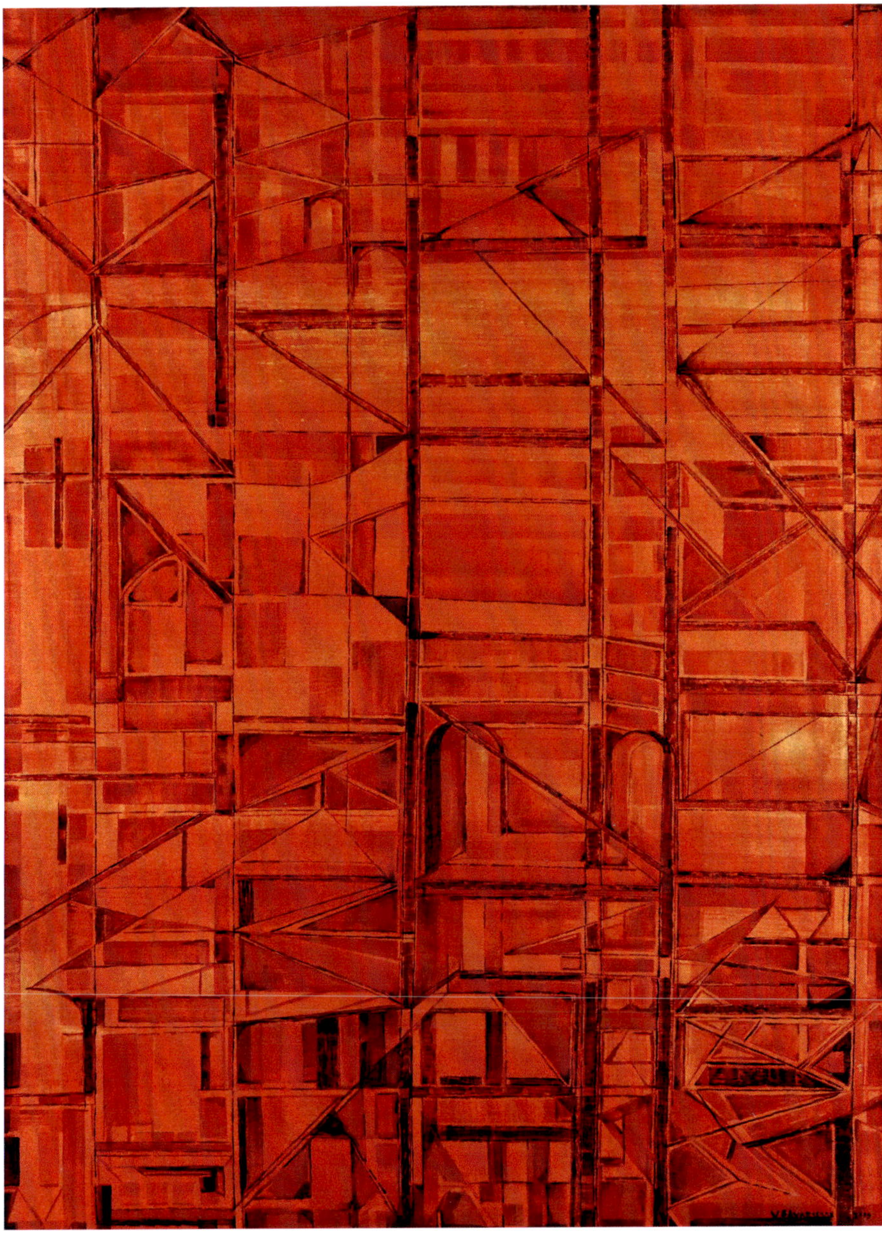

Geometry, Art and Aesthetics

30"x40" • Acrylic on Canvas

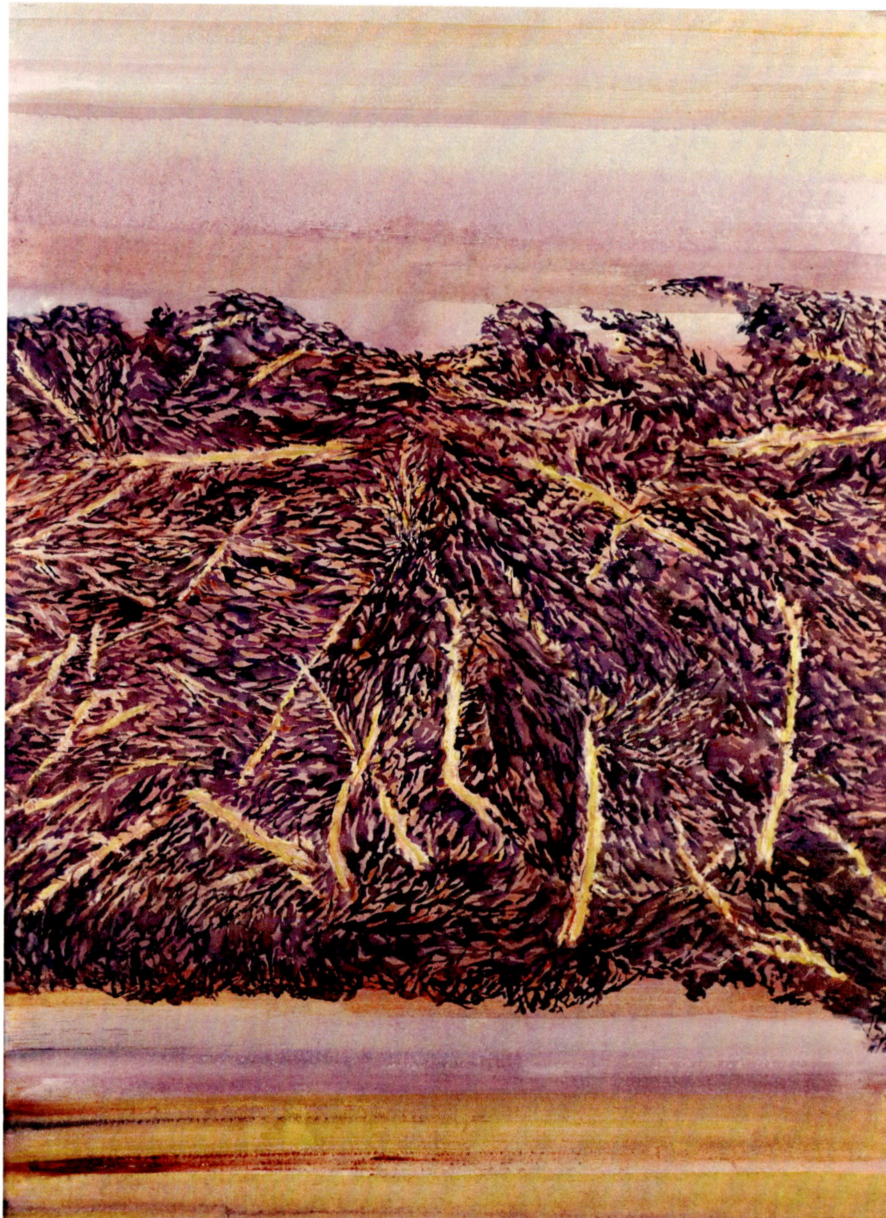

Subconsciousness

30”x40” • Acrylic on Canvas

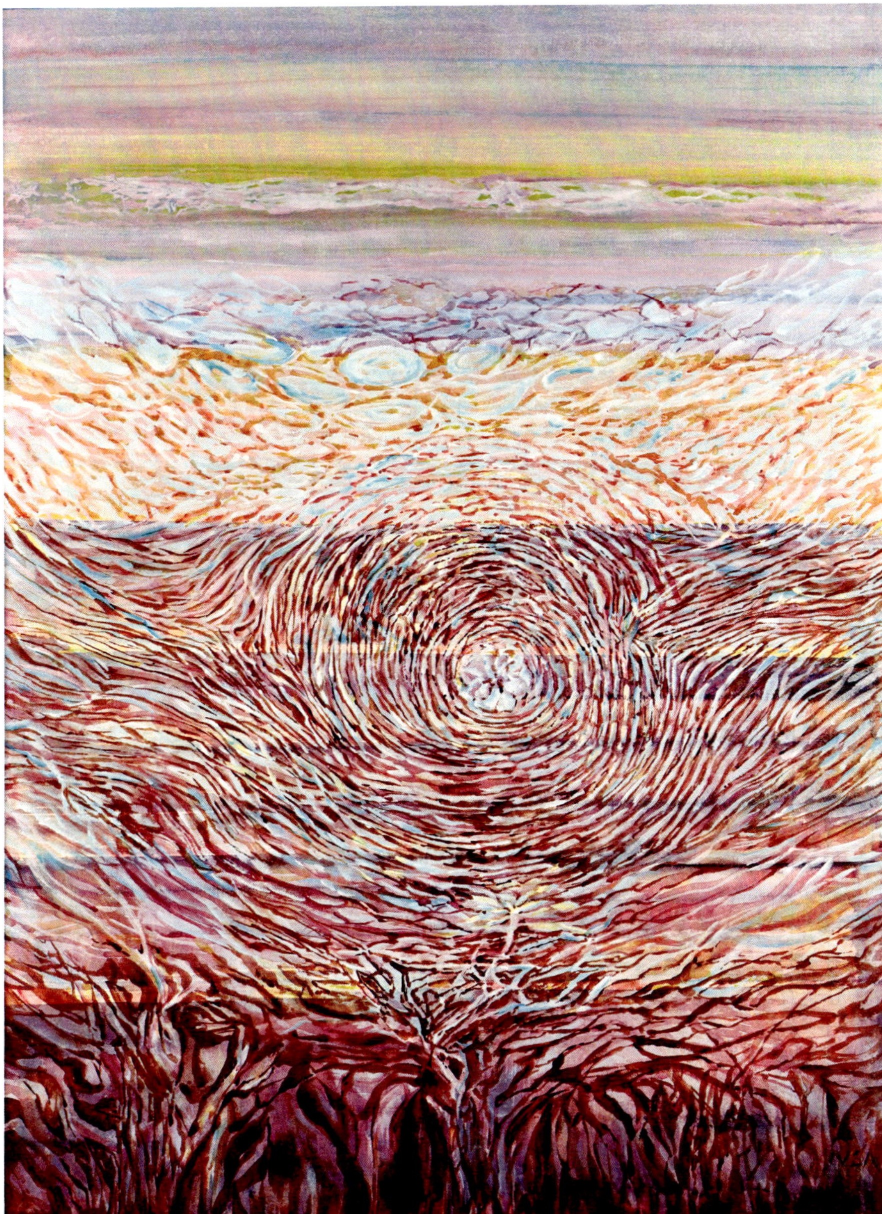

Surge of Consciousness

30"x40" • Acrylic on Canvas

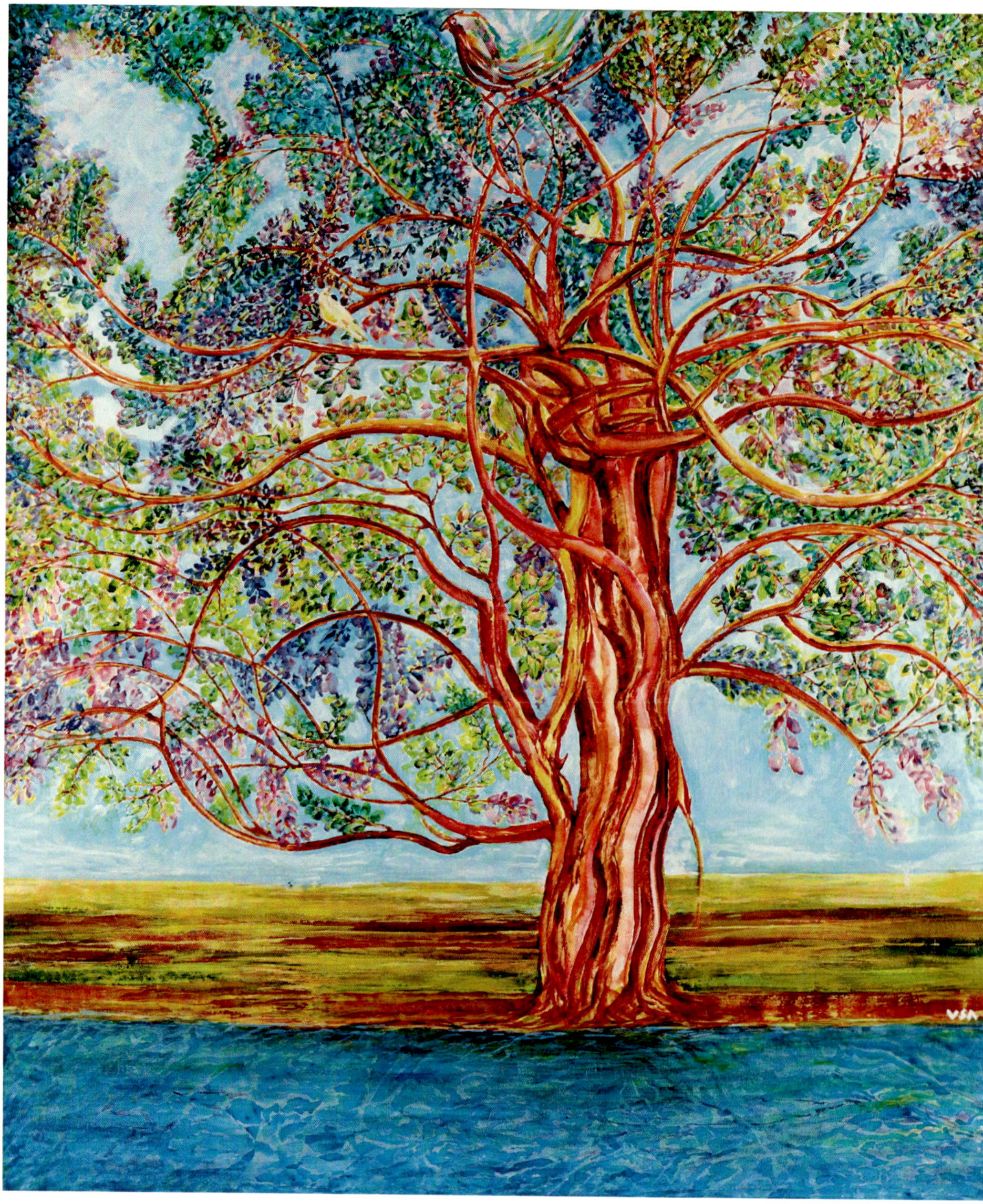

The Tree

36”x42” • Acrylic on Canvas

Fine Art Practices and Meditation

Fine arts include drawing and painting, sculpture and architecture, music, poetry and noble literature. In the evolutionary ascent of human beings, individuals are gifted with different capabilities depending upon their hereditary and environmental factors. Those lucky ones who are involved in the creative work of their choosing will find their activities as uplifting, composing and soothing. Can we compare the creative activities of the fine artists to the spiritual discipline of meditation and contemplations as explained by Swami Chinmayanand?

Polish Philosopher Henryk Skolimowski in his book Let There be Light – says the art of writing is therapeutic, a path to discovery and creation. According to him words and thoughts which produce noble literature are divine vehicles that can lead you to the ultimate light.

Fine art of writing, painting or sculpturing is a gradual, contemplative process towards achieving soul-lifting experience for gifted individuals. The pleasure or joy emanating through such creative activities is known as the aesthetic joy of the beautiful. This can be achieved when the mind is relaxed and the imagination is roaming free, for creative expressions by the artists. Such expressions are achieved by contemplative activities wherein all aspects of the artist's consciousness including id, ego and super consciousness are involved. The disciplines of creative activities of mankind are inclusive of physical, mental and intellectual personality of the individual to kindle life into a harmonious whole. The fundamental principles of all fine arts are to create the harmonious and the beautiful through activities inspired by the artist's natural gifts. Art practice is not necessarily a holistic contemplation where all desires are controlled by the mind. On the contrary the creative process involves dynamic activities of mind and body inspired by imagination, impulsions and skilful practices of the artist. Such activities will enable mankind to ascend in life through work, worship and wisdom.

All disciplines of fine art are distinct creative activities with their characteristic expressions through different mediums employed in their execution. Art of writing is a contemplative gradual process with selective use of words, subtle phrases and simple terms which have specific recognisable meanings. In this discipline, grammar is a must in arrangements of selective phrases to communicate thoughts without any ambiguity. Literary works of artistic merits including epic poetry, lyrics, tragedies and comedies are not strings of speeches expressive of various morals and episodes, but each in itself is a personified organic whole.

In other words, good literature should have unity in plot, individuality and idealisation in order to meet the requisites of fine art. It can then be recognised as noble literature.

Music and Visual Arts

These are two distinct disciplines of fine art. We are aware that the joy of music is experienced through the sense perception of ears and that of visual art through the eyes. Basics of musical compositions are orchestration of the sound with different musical instruments. Music is the language of notes not words nor beats. It is the ultimate in sound. Similarly plastic art – painting and sculpture – is an expression in visual language of perceptions of forms, colours and techniques based on fundamental principles of fine art. There is no need of grammar for either of these art forms. Impulsive and emotional feelings of the artists find expressions in a surge of compositions and designs. The aim and purpose of these two disciplines of fine art are to celebrate universal joy by communion rather than communication. Music and visual arts are abstracts and dynamic in nature and interact instantly with the recipients to give them a unique joy. If you are alert, if you are sensitive and if you are open enough, you are in for a surprise as the mystery of life is before you in creative sight and sound.

Primitive Art

Primitive art of prehistoric cave paintings of Altamira in Spain, and Lascaux in France can be described as art of the senses which delights in liveliness, vitality, sensuous and organic, with animals as important subjects of forms. Its opposite type is Abstract Art. In this type of art there is a tendency to deform the organic forms with a motive, may be religious, symbolic or intellectual. The distinguishing characters of these types of art are known as the expressive forms in the visual art. There is also a possibility that certain forms were created unconsciously by chance and repeated for pleasure and love for creativity. Sometimes, the unconscious 'eye' is a more effective observer than the conscious 'eye'. You may call it instinct or the intuitive faculty of the mind.

General belief is that prehistoric paintings in the dark caves were created for magical purpose. Whatever may be the purpose of such paintings, the pre-requisite condition of their production was the existence of rare individuals of exceptional sensibility and expressive skill. We see in their works prominently those qualities of rhythm, symmetry and vitality, which are specifically aesthetic qualities.

Forms and their Development in Prehistoric Art

A running animal is obviously different in form from a standing one. Form varies with immediate function. A prehistoric artist had sufficient sense to see that vitality and dynamic force are qualities within the object rather than its outer static form. An effective representative art inspired by sympathetic magic was developed by the primitive artists in those dark caves of the prehistoric period.

The vitality of primitive art was due to the close relationship between man and animal. This relationship between the hunter and the hunted, a tense, nervous life of dependence for food and survival, was the basis of the prehistoric man's acquisition of a visual and imaginative conception of the animal world. This in return prepared him for plastic expression of aesthetic vision. Uneven surfaces of the natural cave walls helped the artist to suggest the plasticity in their paintings.

All forms in drawing and painting which are inspired by the world of nature or otherwise, are symbolic like short hand representations of general ideas of objects wherein the emotions associated with them are evoked by the artist. However, two distinct directions in human sensibility i.e. one leading to the abstraction of the word and thought or idea, and the other, to the visual plasticity of the material and form, are clearly noticeable in the history of human development.

The early art of the primitive phase cannot be compared with the art of civilised man of the developed societies. But we must recognise that essentials of art have little or nothing to do with intelligence because creative activity itself is confined to certain gifted individuals who, through special skill in expression, can appeal to the emotions of other individuals. It seems that the forms of animals were first suggested to the caveman, by natural formation or markings of rock surfaces. He then developed this suggestion until he arrived at a close approximation to his mental image of animals. The image making process of a child and the cave man begins by abstracting from visual reality and making graphic outline of an object. They make for representative art which is not an imitation or reproduction, for examples, the 1x2 Altamira and Lascaux Cave paintings.

There are three types of primitive art forms, two of which are geometric and the other one is organic. One of the geometric types of pre-historic art of New Stone Age is abstract symbolic art of the purely ornamental type, which may not be of any high aesthetic standard. But the second type of geometric art of a symbolic nature, produced in response to spiritual requirements of a community, is more significant and of greater aesthetic value than the art expressed in the representational forms.

Art-mysticism and Animism

The word 'mystic' implies belief in forces, influences and actions which though imperceptible to senses are nevertheless real.

There is a clear distinction between the primitive man's belief and practice as against the contemplative faculty or practice by religious men of advanced civilisations. The primitives believed that all objects of sacred character, animate as well as inanimate, were inhabited by a spirit. In such cases, it is not a question of a particular stone being the house of spirit but the stone itself has its spirit and it is alive. Magic and Animism are thus subjective and objective aspects of primitive religion. When religion and art go together, the artist is inclined to serve God by drawing and sculpturing with noble feelings expressive of gratitude. The artist, by virtue of his creative faculty, might have gradually assumed the position and power of a magician. Since magic has been recognised as the origin of science as well as religion, the part played by art in liberation of the general culture of mankind has been fundamental. In contrast to magic which is practical, Animism tends to seek an explanation of events in agents invisible and spiritual. It involves a dualistic world of bodies and souls in their mystic connections. The phenomena of existence of mysterious powers can be conceived only imaginatively. Imagination is thus a key to the art of animistic peoples. Their art is an attempt to symbolise the spirituality behind appearances. There is no attempt to represent any actuality or any living presence. It strives to get beyond the actual to get the transcendental.

In other words, it seeks the reality behind the seeming reality or the invisible behind the visible. Primitive man could achieve this only by abstracting from the reality by seeking an essential structure, a skeletal object. The primitive artist 'geometricised' his representation of the objects, and in this geometric figure found the symbol of the spiritual reality.

Organic and Abstract Art, which is derived from representative and natural objects, seen and remembered, has dominated man's ascent on this planet. In this art there is vitality and power, aesthetic sensibility and its existing contradictions, superstitions and joy, love and hate, confidence and faith. But throughout all these developments of primitive societies to civilisations from the past to the present, aesthetic impulse, like sexual impulse - purposive and expressive, is clearly noticeable.

Art and Religion

The vital energy for artistic interest and artistic creations is universally present and is operative in union with the soul and the emotions. In certain cultural traditions of world civilisations, the main flow of aesthetic energy is poured into religious channels. Different religions of the world have different ritual and ideal concepts for achieving enlightenment and divine bliss. Conceptual rituals, art practices, and creations are bound to be different in form and content to evoke emotions and devotion.

Mysticism survives in human consciousness from prehistoric period to modern times when religion tends to a rational explanation of structure and order of the universe and destiny of mankind. Now, caught up in the process of logical thought, the work of art becomes an intermediary between the world of natural phenomena and the world of spiritual presence. Visual art of temples and churches with their architecture, sculpture and paintings becomes a symbolic vehicle to express mental and emotional states.

Although art is an autonomous activity, civilised religions of the world need to have control for development of religious art. The monumental visual art and architecture of the religious past with their stained glass figurative and geometrical designs to control colourful light from domes and windows, their sculptures, carvings and paintings and statues executed with religious ideology and deep sense of devotion, inspire one and all by their beauty and harmony. The aesthetic value of such art works is not a subject for intellectual apprehension by the spectators. Sculptural carvings of temples in India and China, and the statues of divine ideals of Indian classical periods are most outstanding religious art works in the history of global civilisation. The beholder is spell-bound by the ecstatic and mystic beauty of certain iconic statues which were and are worshipped in the temples of India.

Famous French sculptor Rodin's assertion and appreciation of the Nataraj statue is worth reading in this context. Rodin writes, "The fulfillment of life, the flow of life, the heavens, the sun, the very belief in being and existence is expressed as an overflowing burst of feelings. It is thus that the art of the Far East appears to us! Viewed from a certain profile, the Shiva appears as if reaching towards an infinite end. The expression of the divine nature of human body was attained at that time."

Global Art – Secular

A work of art is valued primarily for what it expresses and not for the manner of expression. Mannerist art does not survive for long. Survival of quality art depends for its survival upon, expressions of ideas and aspirations of a particular historic period, by individuals endowed with exceptional skill and sensibility, to appeal to the aesthetic vision of the present and future generations of the world. To bring a fundamental change in art, the artists need spacious freedom for work. The question before an artist is whether his self-expressed art work should be a marketable commodity – a form of economic servitude – or a spiritual freedom for realisation of his inner joy and truth, through a dynamic meditative and experimental process. This is also a question of development of the artist's own personality. In any case, the artist has to be a humanist first, to celebrate the humanity of his fellow-men.

In this age of developing technology it is easy to visually acquaint oneself with various styles, techniques and art ideas of well known artists of the world. It also pays to study the success and failure of some outstanding artists of the world to develop higher perceptions and inner vision. To grow up as an artist of mature sensibility, study of the history of art, philosophy of art, psychology and general science covering various aspects of nature will be very useful. Knowledge will expand the artist's creative field of vision for discovering and expressing in visual mode the reality of existence.

Artists generally create their works within their limitations of cultural traditions and environments in which they are born. But a genius of exceptional character transcends the traditions by acts of experiment with his insights. Self-consciousness has destroyed the collective spirituality in the modern world, and the artist is forced to seek some form of idealism other than religious superstition.

History of art since the Renaissance (1500-1600 AD) in European countries is the history of various forms of idealism. The renaissance artist tried to review the art of classical Greeks. Therefore, the art practices of the period till 18th century in Europe were based on classical traditions. In the 19th and 20th century, the ideal tenets of art practices were modified on the basis of romanticism and moralism and later individualism was accepted as the ideal basis for art.

In the first half of the 20th century, as a result of World Wars I and II, the entire European World and its social structure were disturbed. People lost their faith in the existing culture of morality and their values. They revolted against everything in life including art, which was considered as one of the great achievements of European nations. Individuals and groups formed by different artists, poets, philosophers, writers and psychologists, came together to bring a change in the existing conditions of life and living. Consequently there was a continual change in the styles, techniques and ideals in the art practices. France was the leading centre for artists and art exhibitions.

French artists Manet and Monet painted impressions of scenes and objects, and their style of paintings was called Impressionism. Thereafter, a number of 'isms' or styles with new ideals named Fauvism, Expressionism, Cubism, Surrealism, Dadaism, Constructivism, Futurism, Suprematism and many more styles ending with Abstract Expressionism or Action Paintings, Op-Art and Pop Art, were seen. By the end of the 20th century we have the extreme form of individualism which would reject all compromise with idealism and depend for its appeal on the bare sensation-ism of form and colour. The artist's freedom for expression in global art is now for the expression of his own inner personality.

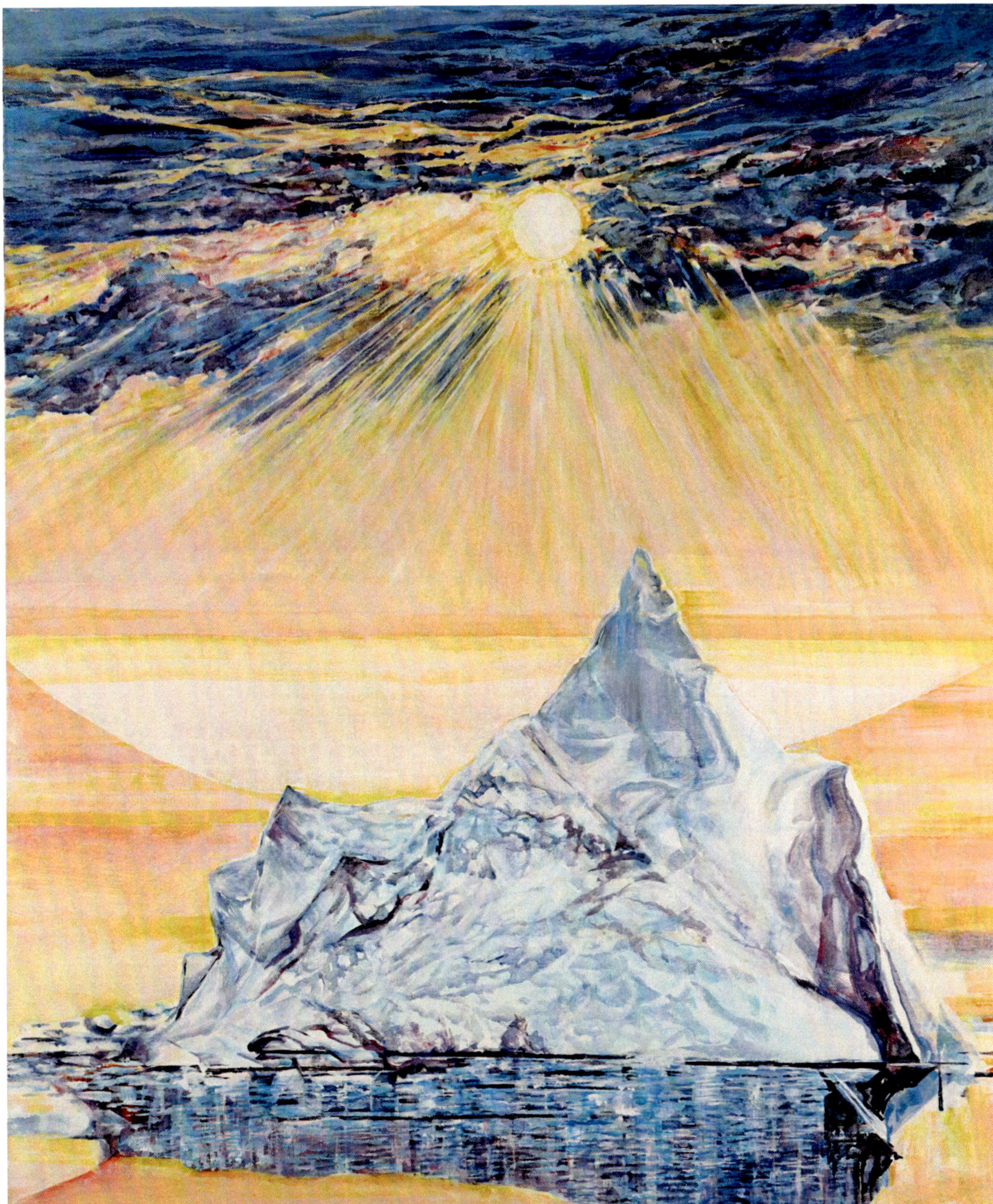

Kailās

30”x40” • Acrylic on Canvas

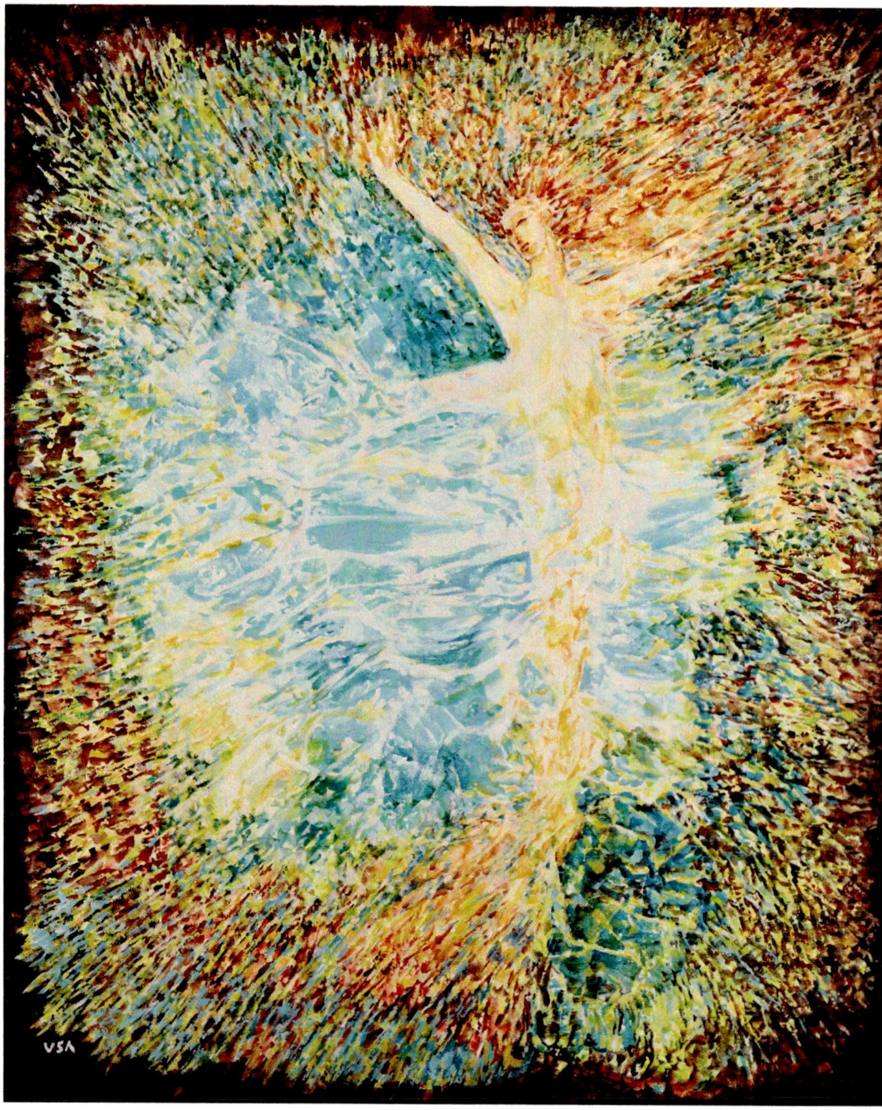

Resurrection

30”x40” • Acrylic on Canvas

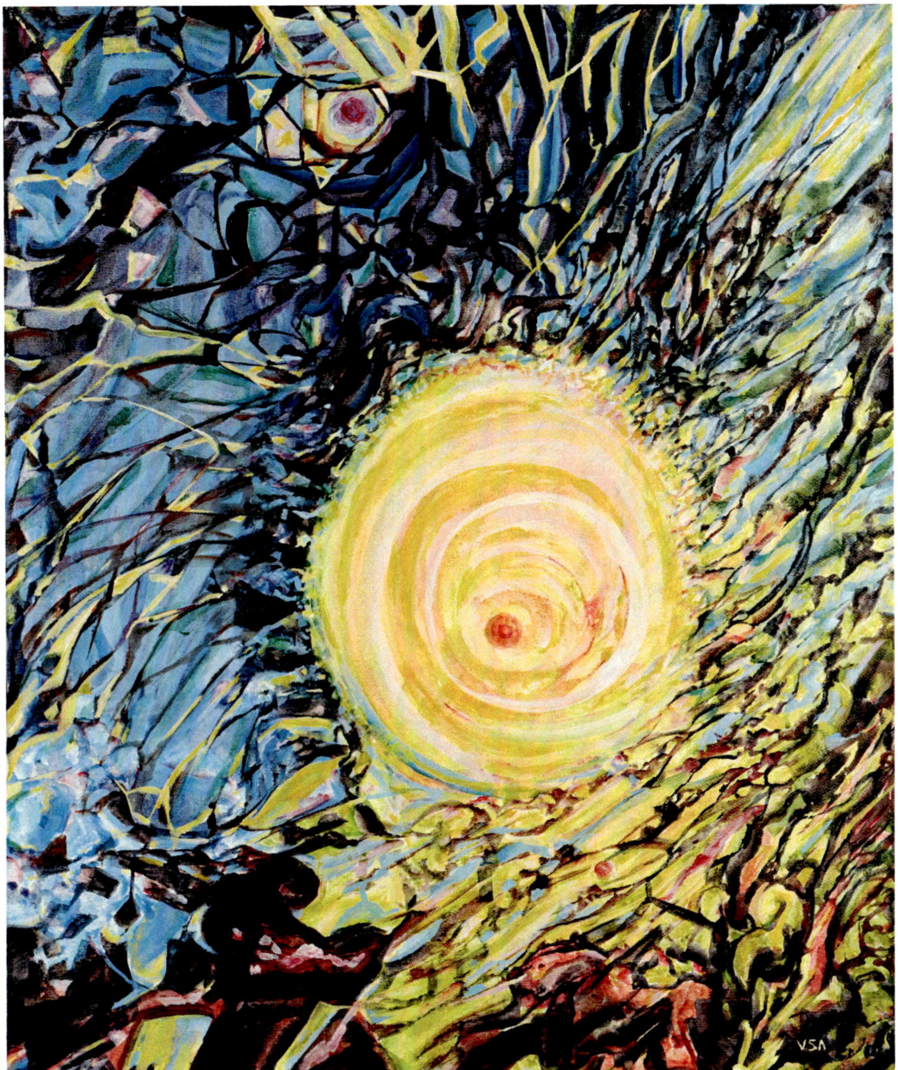

Impact

30”x40” • Acrylic on Canvas

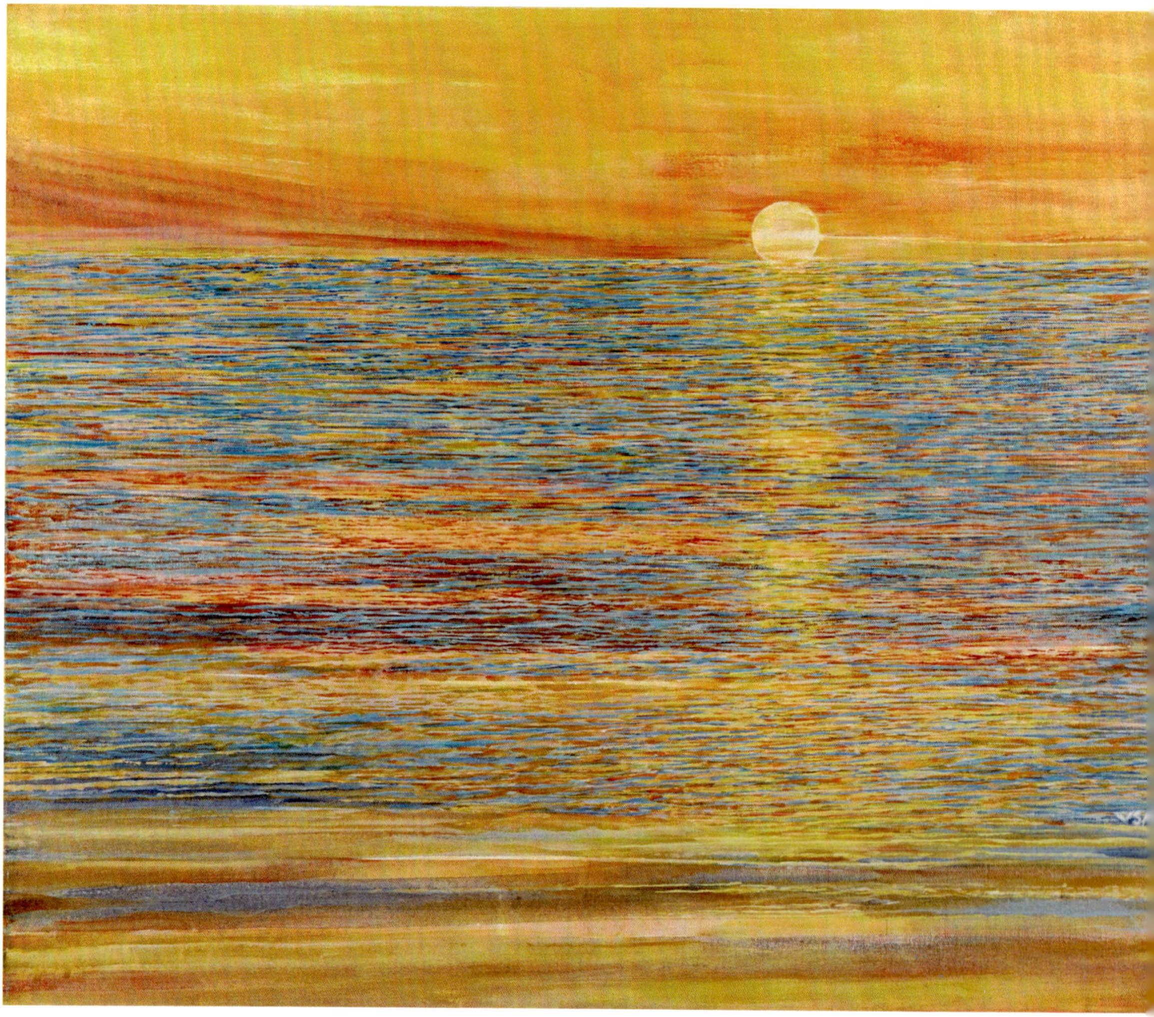

Seascape

40”x30” • Acrylic on Canvas

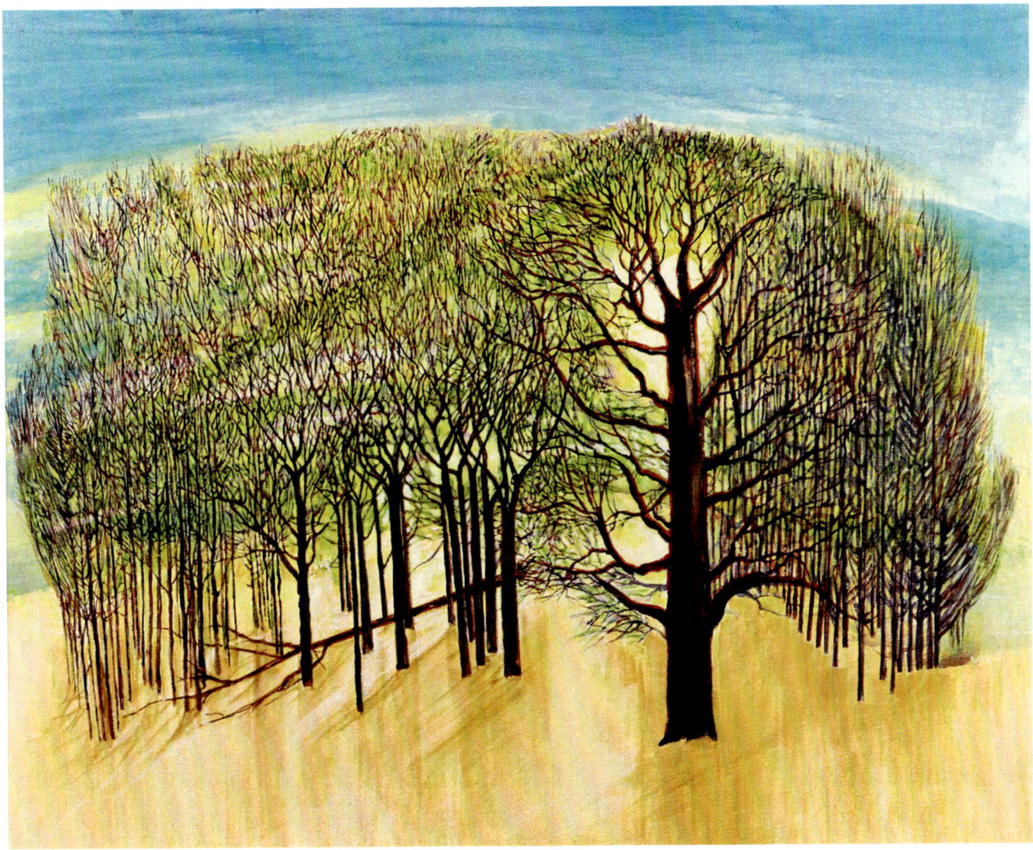

Treescape

30”x24” • Acrylic on Canvas

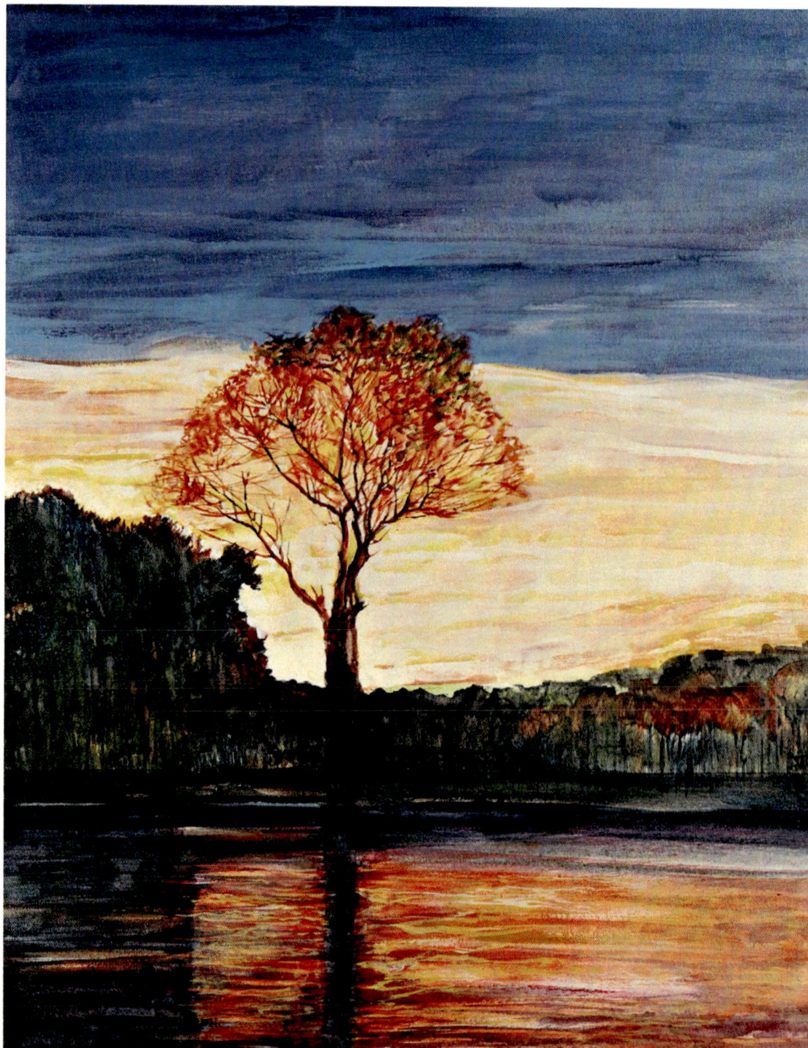

Treescape

24"x30" • Acrylic on Canvas

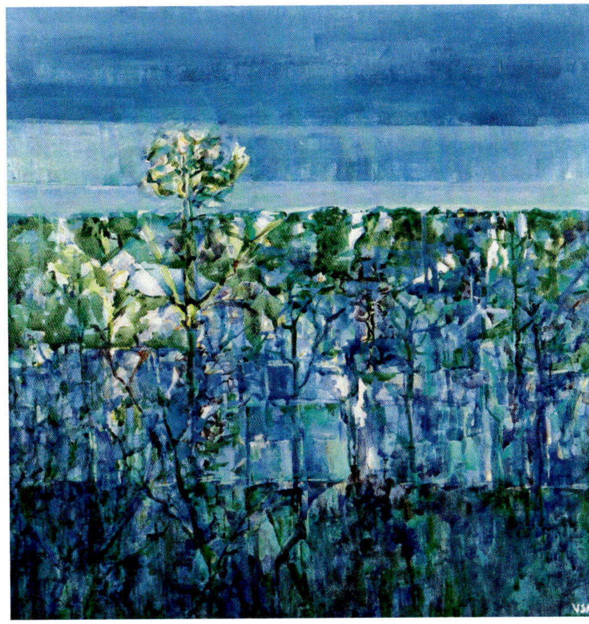

Treescape

21"x21" • Acrylic on Canvas

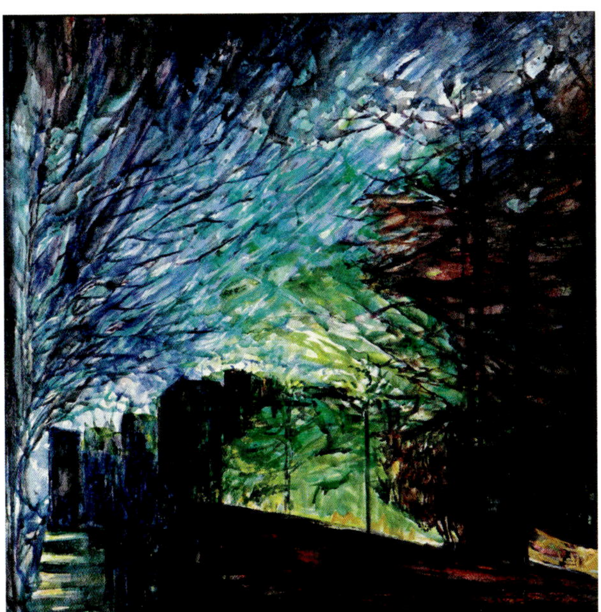

Treescape

21"x21" • Acrylic on Canvas

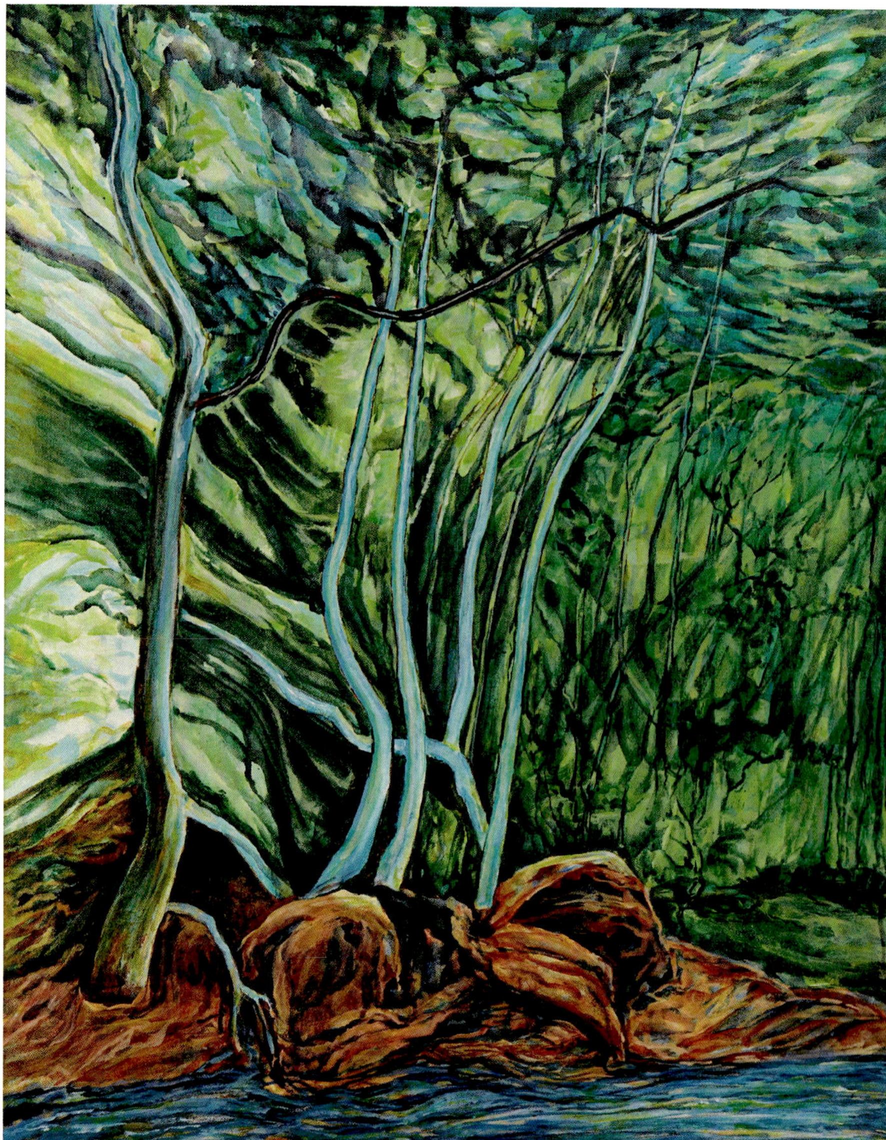

Treescape

24"x32" • Acrylic on Canvas

Origins of Modern Art

Naïvety of styles of some artists of West and East, cannot in any sense, qualify for modern paintings even though some naïve painters like Henri Rousseau and Manjit Bawa have enjoyed considerable reputation among the 20th century artists. Similarly the styles of realistic paintings with some modifications executed with academic traditions of the 19th and 20th century cannot be classified as modern paintings although some of such painters have achieved great accomplishment and permanent value for their works. The style which is specifically known as modern, apart from its variety and complexity, has a unity of intention that completely distinguishes it from the paintings of earlier period of European art. The intention of Modern artist – as explained by Paul Klee of Bauhaus school of Germany, - is not to reflect the visible but to make visible.

Herbert Read, in his book *A Concise History of Modern Painting* writes – "Modern Art, we might say, begins with a father who would have disowned and disinherited his children; it continues by accident and misunderstanding and can only be given coherence by a philosophy of art that defines art in a very positive and decisive manner."

This philosophy defines art as a means of conceiving the world visually. There are many methods of conceiving the world. But art is not to be confused with other alternative methods such as of recorded statements of measurements for scientific and general knowledge. Art is an ever-living question asked of the visual world by visual sense, and the artist is the only person who has the ability and desire to transform his visual perception into material form. The first part of his action is perceptive, the second is expressive. The artist expresses what he perceives and he perceives what he expresses in a simultaneous process.

Art through the ages is therefore a history of modes of visual perception of the various ways in which man has seen the world. The naïve person may believe that there is only one way to see this world – the way it is presented to his own immediate optical vision. But this is not true. We see what we learn to see with a desire to construct a credible world. What we see must be true and real. Art is therefore a process of construction of reality. A universal language to reveal the universal truth.

It is said that modern movement in art begins with the French painter Paul Cezanne who wanted to see the world objectively i.e. he contemplated on the world of objects to become aware visually, of the quality and nature of the objects. His predecessors Manet and Monet had seen the world subjectively, i.e. as it presented itself to their senses in the changing lights of the day and/ or from various points of view. Each occasion made a different and distinct impression on their senses. But Cezanne contemplated on the structures of different objects and his temperament was basically classical, meaning, for a style rooted in the nature of things and not the individual's subjective sensations. Unlike impressionists, Cezanne felt that he could realise his vision of reality by organisation of lines and colours that gave stability and clarity to the image transferred to the canvas. He wanted to paint the objects in the outdoors to apprehend their structure and quality visually without sacrificing the reality and intensity of the image. Cezanne's theory of art was developed and applied in contact with nature i.e. of treating nature "by the cylinder, the sphere, the cone, -everything in proper perspective, so that each side of an object is directed towards a central point. Nature does not preach but to those who train their eyes through contact with her, she teaches. According to Cezanne, there is a culminating point for every object and the edges of objects recede to a centre. This theory of evolution of nature was also explained fully and logically by the ancient Indian philosophers (*Rishis*). According to the ancients, everything in nature emerges from a *bindu* or concentric point, to emerge in varieties of lines, forms, and shapes and finally merge within nature, according to the principles of growth and decay – by cosmic order.

Cezanne declared that light does not exist for the painters. One might say that Cezanne had discovered a contradiction inherent in the very process of art. But the truth of Cezanne's statement lies in the fact that the artist cannot paint light on the canvas without the artificial chiaroscuro, which adds an illusionistic dimension and imitative character to the paintings as seen in the paintings of the earlier centuries.

Cezanne used modulation of colours, meaning the adjustment of one area of colour to the neighbouring areas of colours, a continuous process of reconciliation of different colours for overall unity. This kind of application of colours would not only vibrate with their natural intensity but create colour areas into a mosaic of separate colour-facets. The constituent different planes in the whole picture completely integrated into the picture as a whole without the illusionistic light effects. Cezanne's painting of colour constructs and structures without use of chiaroscuro light effects were free from the illusionistic third dimension and showed the properties of colour and their purity to express the abstract reality. This was a new concept in the development of modern painting. Cezanne's intention was to create an order of art corresponding to the order of nature independent of his own confused sensations. He decided to find a new way to the natural truth by passing beyond romanticism in order to transform it into an enduring art.

Before Cezanne put forward his own thoughts and practice in painting, the French artists were preoccupied with the questions of style or method which they imagined as only true and necessary art of plastic paintings. Their love of reason for everything is misleading because in art, intellect intervenes in the concepts which are sought and the concepts which are found. For this reason we shall never discover the secret of art and the very condition of its origin and life, unless we learn to distinguish between mental processes which take place at conscious, subconscious, unconscious and super conscious levels. The artist being a unit of society with culture needs the basic support of that culture for his progress.

Development of Modern Art in Europe

French artists Henri Matisse and Paul Gauguin, Dutch painter Van Gogh and others revolutionised colour application with direct application of fresh colours, and adapting oriental linear forms in their paintings. Paul Cezanne, was more inventive and was anxious to create new forms of art based on nature. He wanted to show the quality and reality of the objects he painted. His simplification of the forms on the basis of solid geometry and his attempt to show the opposite sides of the objects led to fractured forms in paintings. This is a starting point for Cubism and Modern Art in France. The emphasis upon colour by the Fauves and German Expressionists made it almost logical that the colour by itself without any specific forms constitute the full 'content' of a picture. Russian artist Kandinsky of The Blue Rider group - so called because they liked the colour blue – carried his research into the emotional and psychological properties of colours, lines and shapes where subject matter and even the representational elements were entirely eliminated. In his philosophical treatise "Concerning the Spiritual in Art", Kandinsky proclaimed the independence of colours and their inherent spiritual values. According to him, colours flow on the canvas of a visionary artist as directed by his individual psyche without reference to the objects of the world.

This theory of Kandinsky is comparable to the phenomena of the most fascinating and changing phases of colourful clouds in the skies, particularly at sunrise and sunset, during different seasons of the year. Can we presume that this magical and mystic experience of the percipient is of art without an artist? In this context I would like to assert that all colours are beautiful and the artist's skill, character and discretions are necessary for the power of his expressions. For me, the sky is the abstract canvas of natural elements and forces suggesting Nature's master strokes of abstractions of harmony. The truth of the beautiful is therefore the existence of our aesthetic consciousness.

History of art reveals that Kandinsky's treatise and Freud's conclusions concerning subconscious and dream images were exploited by Surrealists like Dali and others.

Cubism and its Influence on Modern Art

Pablo Picasso, the Spanish painter who had established himself in France, was gifted with skills and powers of pictorial visualisation. His constant experimentation and shifts from one kind of painting to another, art ideas and innovations made him a successful artist of his time. Picasso and Braque, a French artist, together created a new style of painting called Cubism. In their pictorial designs, objects were painted as if seen from several different angles with more or less geometrical forms of objects conceived earlier by Cezanne. Cubist's pictorial space suggests addition of new dimensions of time and space since the objects are shown not as seen at any one moment but in temporal sequences. Analytic and synthetic Cubism is an attempt to show objects of multi-dimensions on two dimensional surface of canvas with many parts and points of objects in one composition. Thus, for the first time Cubism had broken the renaissance structure of fixed appearance into limitless world of forms. This was a starting point of discussions regarding relevance of abstract forms of art and its relationship to the natural forms from which such abstract forms were derived, consciously or subconsciously, by the artists. Varied answers to these questions have led to the proliferation of many schools and styles or 'ism' in Modern Art.

As a reaction to the Cubist's complex and intricate forms in art descending from Cezanne's geometric view of nature, artists like Kazimir Malevich and Mondrian moved towards geometrical forms through their designs of simplicity and balance, symmetrical and asymmetrical. Such designs are now in common use in modern architecture of simplistic beauty.

Constructivists Naum Gabo and Pevsner created new art forms with modern materials such as sheet metal, wires, plastics etc, which were readily accepted in modern sculptures and constructions. There was clarity and order in their art forms reflecting modern culture and developing technology.

Dadaism to Surrealism

Duchamp, the French artist, was the leader of a group of artists and their art style was named Dadaism. Dadaists were against the constructive and disciplined attitude towards all existing art practice. Their philosophy of art was fundamentally nihilistic – non-art or anti-art in kind. Duchamp did not believe in organised art practice of various styles and wrote destructive criticism against such art. According to his philosophy, Dada was a metaphysical attitude – a way to get out of a state of one's mindset. Individual freedom can be achieved only by avoiding the influence of one's environment. Frankly speaking, this is an attempt to escape from conventional forms and modes of expressions. This art movement came to a sudden end in the year 1922. Consequently, this art movement also paved a way for freedom of art practice of absurdity, and gimmicks, but justified the metaphysical in paintings of fantasy and dream images, for example, (i) 'The Persistence of Memory' by Salvador Dali (Surrealist), (ii) 'Delights of a Poet' by De Chirico (Metaphysical) and (iii) 'Crucifixion' by Marc Chagall (Fantasy).

The artist's free imagination now draws upon material lying deep in his consciousness, and his act of expression is the proclamation of new realities, not less real because they are psychic. In the psychoanalytic view of Freud and other psychologists, art is a powerfully practical means of self-revelation, and the images that rise out of subconsciousness or dream images have a truth of their own independent of the world of conventional vision. The new type of fantastic paintings referred to above came into existence almost at the same time as Cubism but were entirely different in concepts. The metaphysical paintings created by De Chirico became a source of inspiration for the artists who created the Surrealist movement in the early 1920's.

The Surrealist's intention and aim, as formulated in their manifesto, were to resolve 'conscious and subconscious' reality into a new and absolute reality – a super-reality (Surrealistic) ie. 'to re-establish man as psychology instead of anatomy'. They wanted to bring in their paintings and constructions the aspects of outer and inner reality in a single composition. The images or the projection in visual form of this new conception required new techniques. Surrealists adopted some of the Dadaist devices but with new purposes. In order to project the world of dreams as convincingly as possible, artist Salvador Dali restudied the realistic masters of the earlier period. Since in dreams, objects and situations collide and interpenetrate in an endless metamorphosis. Dali used multiple images of multiple symbolic meaning to suggest evocations from his subconscious. He had also developed a fundamental Surrealist method of painting by juxtaposition of seemingly irrelevant and certainly unrelated objects in unexpected situations. The surprise effect to Dali's work depends upon his presentation of absurdities in a meticulous miniature like technique.

These several aspects of his style and technique to show dream images of subconscious can be seen in his most familiar work, 'Persistence of Memory'.

Modern Art after World War II

After the end of World War II, traditional values of organised modern life were challenged and criticised. Art had become big business, and ambitious commercially minded galleries continued to tighten their hold on artists. Since then works of art have become a commodity in the art market, and modern advertising has been promoting it. The works so selected for promotion of art only show certain modern trends of fashion and novelty. Such art works without the essence and soul of creative characteristics may not have the quality of excellence of fine art. Pop and Neo-Dadaist cultures of modernists have adverse effects on fine art practices of the present generation. Art is sensuous and seductive. The very fact that it has such power over the feelings and imagination is the reason why it must be rigorously controlled for its own survival as well as spiritual health of future generations.

The minimal art works in the modern world sometimes draw the maximum attention and price. The artist has only to set a new trend. Consider the famous example of American artist Jackson Pollock who used to walk in a drunken trance over large canvases spread on the ground, throwing and spilling enamel paints on them directly with the painting can, and there after making some changes with brush strokes.

Pollock named his style and process of dancing and painting as Action Painting, since his whole body and mind worked in a hypnotic trance to the background music while he was painting. The resultant works, and style was also named as Abstract Expressionism. If Pollock's painting is an image of anything, it is the process itself in its never ending creation of nature's endless and intricate forms and colours. A large size canvas spattered with bright enamel and aluminum colours everywhere is bound to give some magical and amazing visual effects. Kandinsky's treatise on spiritual art has come to a final state in the history of American Modern Art. The art market in America has given maximum price to such paintings.

In India, people celebrate on a particular day of every year a festival of colours when people come outdoors and take part in dancing and sprinkling colours on each other, called Ranga Panchami. This is a religious and social gathering when colours are liberally thrown on each other by males and females without any hesitation or planning. The joy of colours is for all and India is known for her spiritual tradition. However, this process is yet to be recognised creation of Abstract Art.

I think fashionable evolution has given rise to the new fashionable forms of glorification. But all such forms of art may not qualify for excellence in fine art.

POP or Popular Art

Pop or popular art exists in various forms including advertisements of motor cars and bikes, films and sports, hoardings and fashionable garments. Pop Art is always diffused, appealing to the tastes of the wider public. It is not recognised as fine art either at the time of its creation nor thereafter, because it always changes depending upon the times and tastes of the masses and forsakes the aesthetic and moral basis of its activities. After Abstract Expressionism, in late fifties, Pop Art had a striking resemblance both in attitude and method, to Dada and is also called Neo-Dada. Pop Art like pop-music is factual and not symbolic.

A fine artist depends for his progress in art on his concepts and convictions. It may be said that a fine artist can create only one masterpiece in his lifetime. In this kind of art work one can observe artistic excellence of subtlety, suggestivity, simplicity and the masterly skills of presenting or expressing beautiful truth. On the other hand popular and Neo-Dada art is produced with specific intention to reach common people either for advertising or entertainment. It is competitive in nature and therefore comparative, unlike fine art and its artists.

Concepts of Modern Art

In the concepts of Modern Art, apart from understanding the nature of aesthetic impulse, one should be aware of a whole series of phenomena

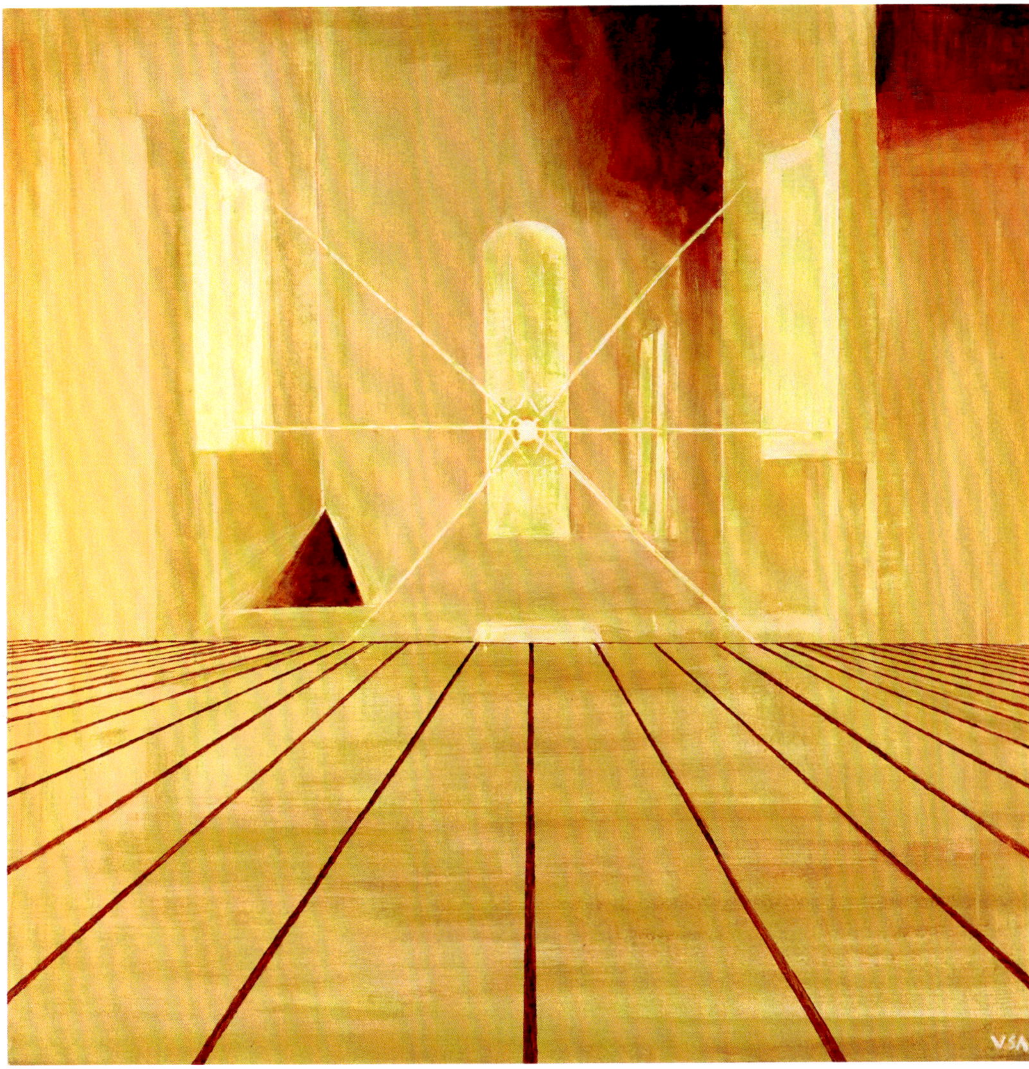

Contemplation for Meditation

36"x36" • Acrylic on Canvas

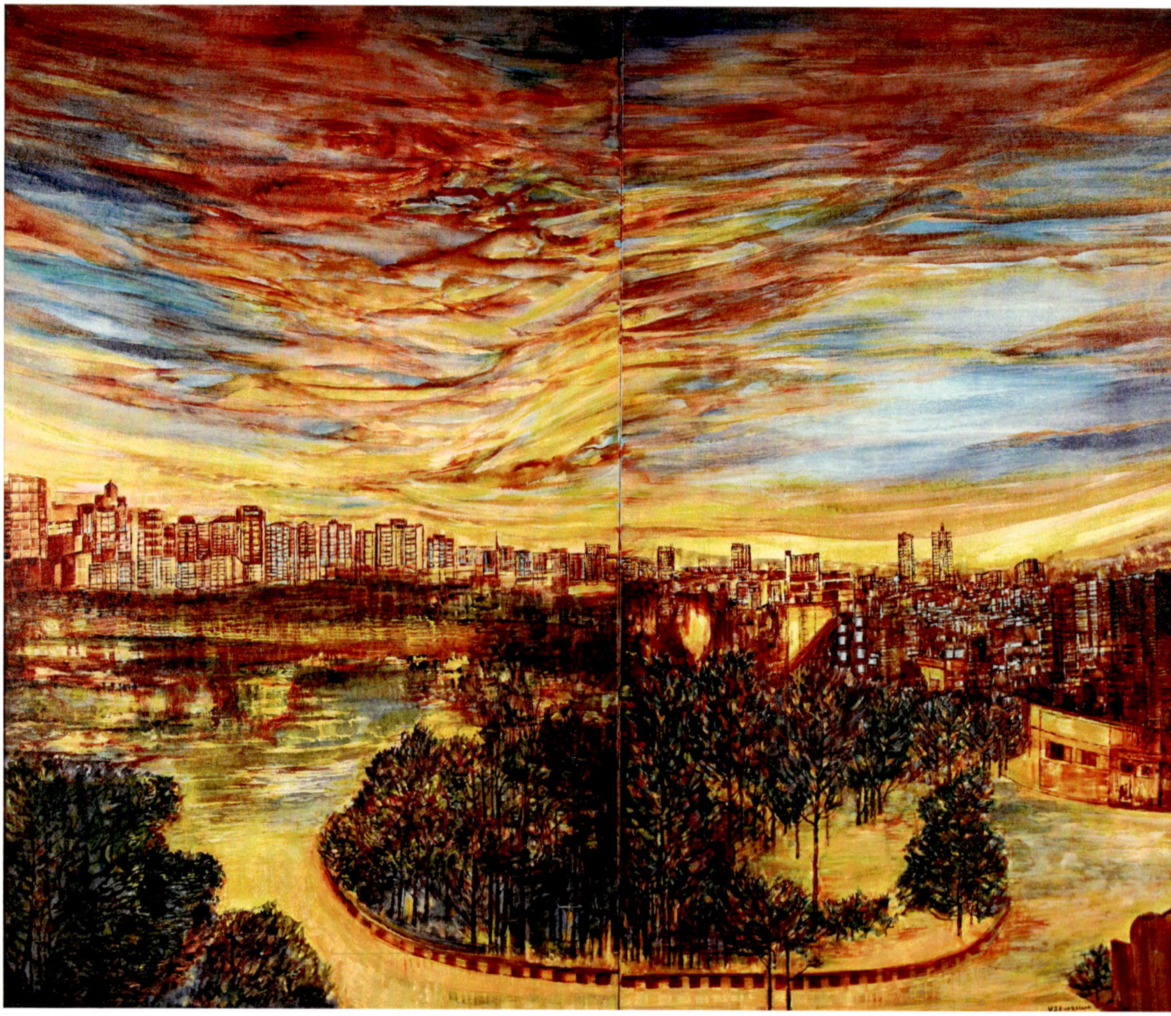

Sky and the City

60”x48” • Acrylic on Canvas

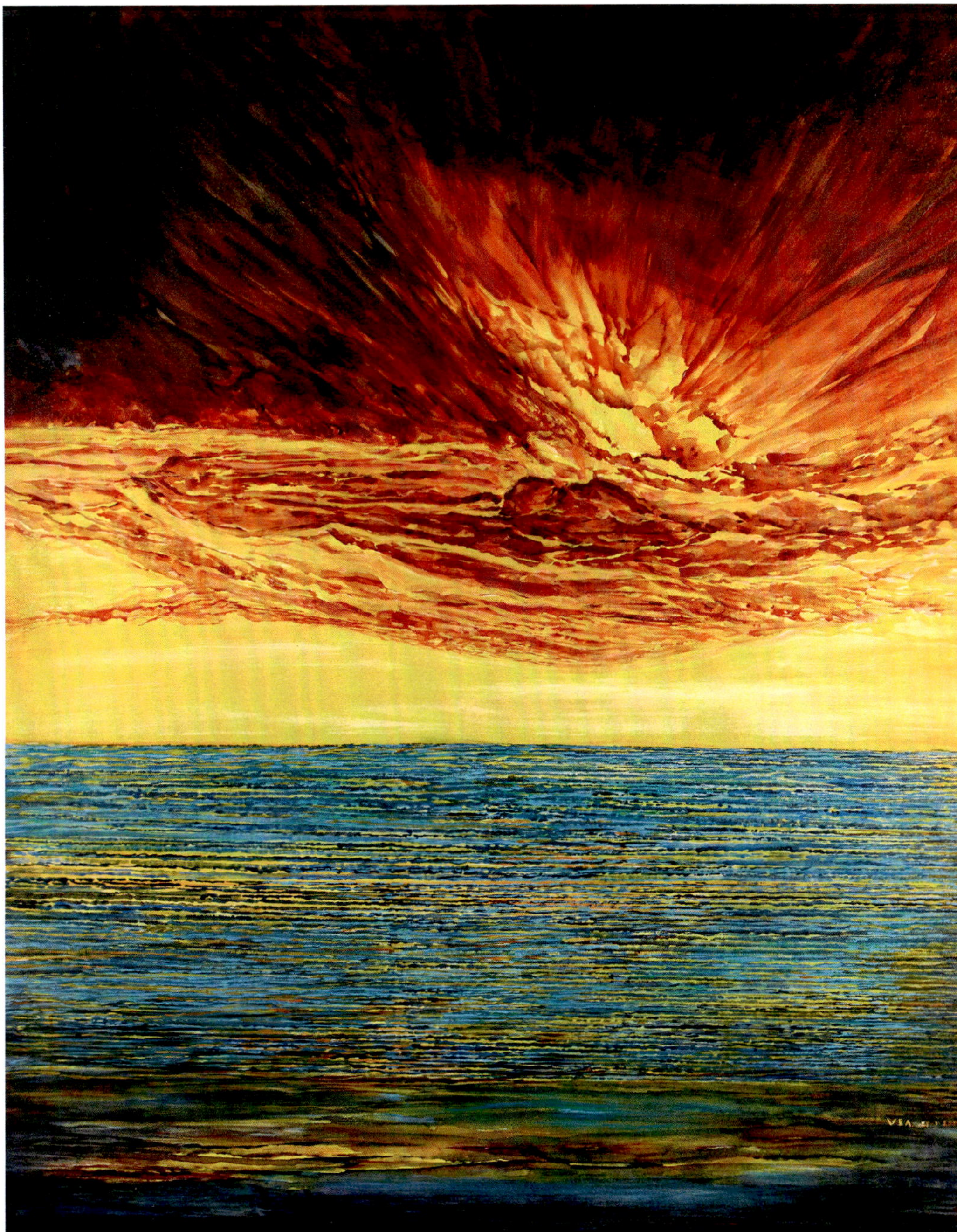

Sky and the Sea

48"x60" • Acrylic on Canvas

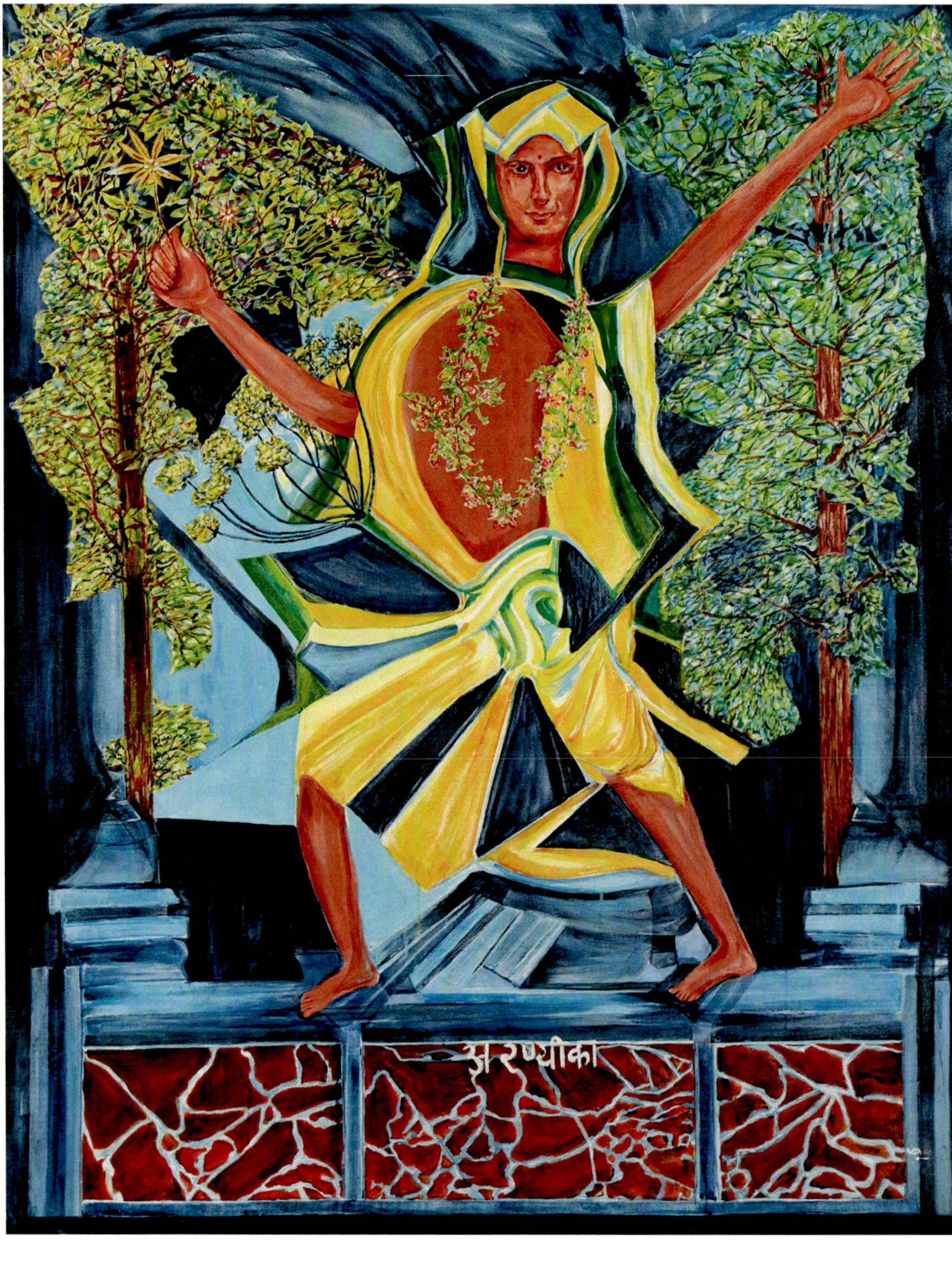

Aranyika (Tree-Goddess)

48”x60” • Acrylic on Canvas

– magic, mysticism, symbolism, religious emotions, moralism, rationalism and irrationalism, if any. For this purpose, the persons concerned need the knowledge of psychology and philosophy of individual in relation to social groups. In addition to social and cultural uses of art objects, art is a profoundly significant factor to any psychological approach to the problems of human society. In the modern world of technological advance and growing tension, the psychoanalysis based on Freud's theories may be accepted as key to most of the unsolved problems of art.

The work of art has its origin in the consciousness of an individual. The artist can and does create a work of art for himself. But he needs the approval of the society and its acceptance of his work for his full satisfaction. Normally the community does not and is not in a position to sit in conscious judgment over works of art. History of art can provide enough evidence to prove this point.

(i) Dutch artist Vincent Van Gogh could not sell a single painting in his lifetime even though his brother was an art dealer at that time. Being hyper-sensitive and extremely emotional to the point of nervous breakdown, his frustration in life led him to commit suicide.

(ii) The French artist Paul Gauguin and his art works were sharply criticised by the community during his stay in Paris. He left his country forever to settle in Tahiti. He created his paintings alone in different cultural environments. Decades after the death of such artists, their works have been collected and auctioned for millions of dollars. These historical facts reveal that human consciousness or/and psychological states of artists and society play an important role depending upon time and traditions of a particular country as well as conditions of economic phases of development.

Modern psychologists have admitted that group psychology is distinct from individual psychology. This is also applicable within the sphere of art. An individual is born with innate characteristics. But these characteristics are modified in scope and direction by infantile experiences. Freud believed that aesthetic pleasure produced in the beholder of art works by a creative artist is only of the preliminary character and that the real enjoyment of a work of art is due to the ease and relief it gives to certain psychic tensions.

According to Freud there are three levels of consciousness: the ego, the superego and the id. The 'id' is the obscure, inaccessible part of our ego and personality. In the 'id' there is nothing corresponding to the idea of time or recognition of the passage of time. The 'id' knows no values, no good and evil, no morality. The existence of 'id' can be confirmed only from the dreams and psycho-analysis of individuals.

Super-ego, according to Freud, is that part of conscience which holds up ideals. It advocates morality in thoughts and actions, perfections in practices, which we call the higher things in human life.

The work of art communicates with each region of the mind. It derives its energy and its mysterious powers from the 'id' which is to be regarded as the source of inspiration. It is given formal synthesis and unity by ego. Super-ego is responsible for ideologies or spiritual aspirations of the artist depending upon his characteristic personality.

In the process of creation, the artist is not aware of time. The sensational awareness of the ego of the artist comes in direct contact with his 'id', supplying him with archetypal forms and images which constitute the basis of art work. Individuals recognised as artists in all ages have natures' gift and possess requisite inspiration, intuition, imagination and skill. Such artists with unique faculties have the capacity to materialise instinctual life of the deepest level. They are also mystics in a way and exercise eternal influence with objective representations.

Art Education - A Discipline

In my experience of 25 years of teaching subjects like history of art, aesthetics, drawing and painting and art appreciation at Sir J.J. School of Art, Mumbai, I became aware that the art students with essential knowledge and definitions of terms and ideas, thoughts and facts of art history, could not easily recognise the good art works from the bad. The best I could do was project on a large screen the paintings and sculptures of major artists of the world and discuss the merits, successes and failures of artist's works rendered at different stages of life and their cultural environments. Students' participation in discussions was made compulsory. I could get the positive responses and expressions of joy of encountering meritorious art works only from very sensitive students of distinct sensibility and curiosity which is prerequisite for good creations. I am convinced that without such distinct aesthetic sensibility it is very difficult to choose good works of fine art from the bad.

Artist Raza who is a J.J. alumnus, lived and practiced in the west to become a famous professional artist. After settling down in India, in one of his lectures arranged by me at J.J. School of Art, he proclaimed that all forms emerge from a *bindu* or point. His belief and practice after his return to his country are based on an ancient Indian philosophic treatise. Later he declared that he found a new icon for his art practice and that all his paintings of earlier period need to be discarded. This means that the artist is ever growing and changing in styles and techniques with his philosophy and psychology as basis for his expression. An artist's permanent asset is in his distinct sensibility, skills, colour sense and visual concepts. Presumably for this very reason, artist Tyeb Mehta had declared that it is necessary for an artist to continue his work as long as he lives.

Tyeb Mehta, also a J.J. alumnus, lived and created paintings in India. His flowing creative lines in the compositions of very unique nature showed Indian-ness in the simplicity of bold and beautiful colour contrasts and their application without use of chiaroscuro. Many aspects of modernity and distortions are used to emphasise the emotional contents of the symbols, mythical and personal. His highly priced paintings of Indian mythology like 'Mahishasura & Kali' have not hurt the feelings of any particular society because he was a humanist and artist. During my teaching profession of higher art at Sir J.J. School of Art, I had the opportunity to meet many contemporary artists and art teachers of India. But I cannot forget the living memories of two sensitive talents of Sir J.J. School of Art. They are Professor Shankar Palsikar and V.S. Gaitonde, who worked together to create a J.J. Style of experimental Indian figurative art compositions.

Professor Palsikar, the Dean of Sir J.J. School of Art, was a philosopher artist. During a discussion on art syllabus he mentioned to me that art students should be both sensitive and inquisitive. In addition to history of art, they should acquire knowledge in all subjects including religion, science, biology, philosophy and psychology for their introspection and growth in their art practices. I agreed and said that artists without inner voice and intuition can hardly realise and reveal the abstract and universal truth behind the seeming realities of the world of nature.

I referred to Swami Vivekanand's statement that in the world of Maya(transcendental world) there is God. That truth is to be discovered by an individual artist with true knowledge and experience. The intention of the Modern artist is to express the universal truth in a visible mode appealing to the conscience of observers and art promoters. The artist, like pure scientists, experimentally develops his own technique and style for his expressions. For him, his work is both worship and award. His basis, and the source of his fountainhead, is the world of nature and her elements.

Professor Palsikar mastered the art of figurative compositions and excelled in portraiture.

The art of portraiture is not a mirror image or reflection of nature as some modernists believe. It is an abstraction unfolding the mystery of life of body and soul by using accurate observations of structural characteristics of the individuals and their personalities. The portrait of Mona Lisa painted in oil on panel by Leonardo da Vinci, was considered to be a masterpiece among the world's most famous portraits. Mona Lisa is shown in half-length view, her hands folded and her gaze directed at the observer. This painting was held in high esteem by artists and critics for nearly 4 centuries, i.e. till the beginning of Modern Art and Dadaism of 20th century, when this fine art was defaced.

Leonardo da Vinci as an artist scientist who worked hard to discover the laws underlying the flux and process of nature. With this end in mind he contributed to our knowledge of physiology and psychology, by studying the changing images of reality through its process of growth and decay. He believed that the scientific investigation can make him a better artist. He invented a new technique of colour application by using many layers of thin oil-colours, one over the other, so that the shades and lights fused to create a vaporous atmospheric chiaroscuro. His superb skill in drawing and painting created the enigmatic face of Mona Lisa with a mysterious smile on it.

As a professor and Dean of Sir J.J. School of Art, Palsikar was often called upon to give demonstrations in portrait painting. In one of his demonstrations it was revealed to my mind that Professor Palsikar was a modernist and a master of portraiture with his own technique. His style and technique were bold and precise to capture the unique personality of the individual before him. As a philosopher artist he had empathy for every individual. His portraits depicted the beauty of the mind within a body apart from the likeness of the individual. He dared to gaze into the eyes of the models to have a glimpse of their inner life. His portraits of the ugly were beautiful and that of the beautiful, even more beautiful.

Artist V.S. Gaitonde was essentially experimentalist by nature. His 'Portrait of a Woman' (in the collection of Sir J.J. School) is a geometrically simplified symbolic image. His subsequent works are path-breaking experiments with colours and forms to seek unity in a variety of visual arrangements, resulting in abstract expressions of beauty in simplicity. His later works suggest his unmatched accomplishments in achieving unison with subjective and objective reality of existence. His suspended colour space with intriguing and sometimes non-recognisable forms submerged in the background; give a visual sensation of mysticism and contemplation of the unknown.

Painting and Sculpture

Painting, sculpture and architecture constitute separate disciplines of visual art, but they often integrate and supplement each other. With advances in technology new substances have been developed and are being used in the creative activities of this century.

Drawings, paintings and graphic arts including lithography are almost wholly two dimensional when created on plane surfaces of papers, canvases or flat surfaces of wooden panels and plastered walls. The painter's concern is essentially to create multifaceted images on two dimensional surfaces with colours, forms and techniques. It can be said that, to some extent illusion has been a necessary element of every art form. But some Modern artists namely Piet Mondrian, Kazimir Malevich and Kandinsky renounced all representational elements in their paintings to create Abstract Art of pure basic forms with limited colours. Their two dimensional designs were created with the belief that true abstract reality is attained through dynamic movement in equilibrium. With straight lines, triangles, squares, and rectangles, artist Mondrian created two-dimensional designs arranged in such subtle asymmetrical balances of line, colour and area that even slight changes would destroy the composition. Mondrian adjusted the design so carefully that no single portion of the surface was more important than the other.

His compositions of aesthetic visual balances were created to express a clear vision of reality. There were no representations of the objects of the world and therefore no illusions in his compositions. His works are the creations and expressions of pure aesthetic emotions. Such art works are based on contemplative meditation on basic forms and pure colours. It is a distinct spiritual discipline to achieve aesthetic visions in rhythms and balances of asymmetrical and symmetrical forms.

The fundamental question of modern life and art in the 20th century was "What is real? Where nothing is certain and everything is questionable". In the view of modernists, art was redefined as the free manipulation of its elements and arrangements that need no reference to anything outside it, which is to say, it need not represent anything. The Modern artist, like the scientist, experiments with his medium, investigates its possibilities and discovers new forms.

But while defining Modern Art the philosopher-artists of the 20th century have forgotten the fact that the function of fine art is to fulfill the requirements of emotional as well as spiritual life of mankind. Experimental sciences and their technologies have discovered the abstract forces of nature to serve mankind for material development on this planet. Thus the experiments in science and art stand apart. Art is for development of human personality with expressions of his emotional life and love which is the essence of his existence. It is no wonder that, as Modern Art had developed through its many movements, the general public, most often, had been rather hostile to it.

Creative artists of the 21st century have much to learn from the dangerous and confused art world of the 20th century. In any case, being independent and not affected by any groups, the artist of the 21st century is free to experiment with his concepts to find the means of expression of his insights. He is expected to reconstruct reality from his own private experience.

All forms and shapes and structures in nature are functional and viable, because nature has created them with the principle of dynamic reality, which we call life. Modern science and technologies have discovered invisible and abstract forces of our cosmic planet. Designers of modern Industrial products have cleverly accepted some functional forms from nature, for example, forms of birds in flight for aircraft design. Nature teaches without preaching and inspires the artists within us to create a new visible world of its own. This is the abstract reality of our imaginative and contemplative mind. But the modern painters and sculptors of the 20th century after the World Wars discarded nature's visible forms, thinking that such practices would be an imitative process in creative art. Now, the question is how the artists should express visually their sentiments and feelings of attachment to the visual world in which they live? As a matter of fact, in paintings, visual symbolic forms are both means and contents of visual expressions. The revolutionary artists who were against all the traditional forms of European culture and art resorted to distortions of natural forms, figures and their proportions including the perspective in their paintings. They exhibited the revolutionary characteristics of their time. Many styles and techniques of Abstract Arts were innovated, discussed and accepted by the modernist groups consisting of artists, philosophers and psychologists. Dr. Freud's research and findings in abnormal psychology, and his revelations of conscious and subconscious mind provided material for new concepts to some artists who wanted to show the reality behind the seeming reality of the objects of the world. For example, French artist Salvador Dali's painting, 'The Persistence of Memory', is an outstanding example of dream images of the Surrealist style and technique. Thus the modern European artists began to penetrate nature's secret truth on the basis of philosophy and psychology. The Western artists and art historians who were initially critical about the Indian metaphysical expressions in spiritual art of the Indian temples, began to appreciate the traditional Indian art.

While the development of Modern Art through the 20th century made the world artists independent and free from any restrictions of styles, techniques and concepts, artists should however be careful not to hurt the religious feelings of the people of the world with the assumption that artists have unbridled freedom of expressions. A creative artist is a respected individual of society and the country of his birth. He is therefore responsible with his personal talents, to create suitable environmental conditions for growth and evolution of social and spiritual life on this planet. It is unhealthy for the future of art, if some of the talented artists consider themselves as professionals, and produce art works only with an eye on the art markets.

Traditional Indian Art

My retrospection and review of visual art will remain incomplete if it fails to point out some salient features of ancient Indian paintings and sculptures which span more than 20 centuries of history in the subcontinent. History of Indian paintings goes back to a few centuries BC. Paintings of Ajanta, which

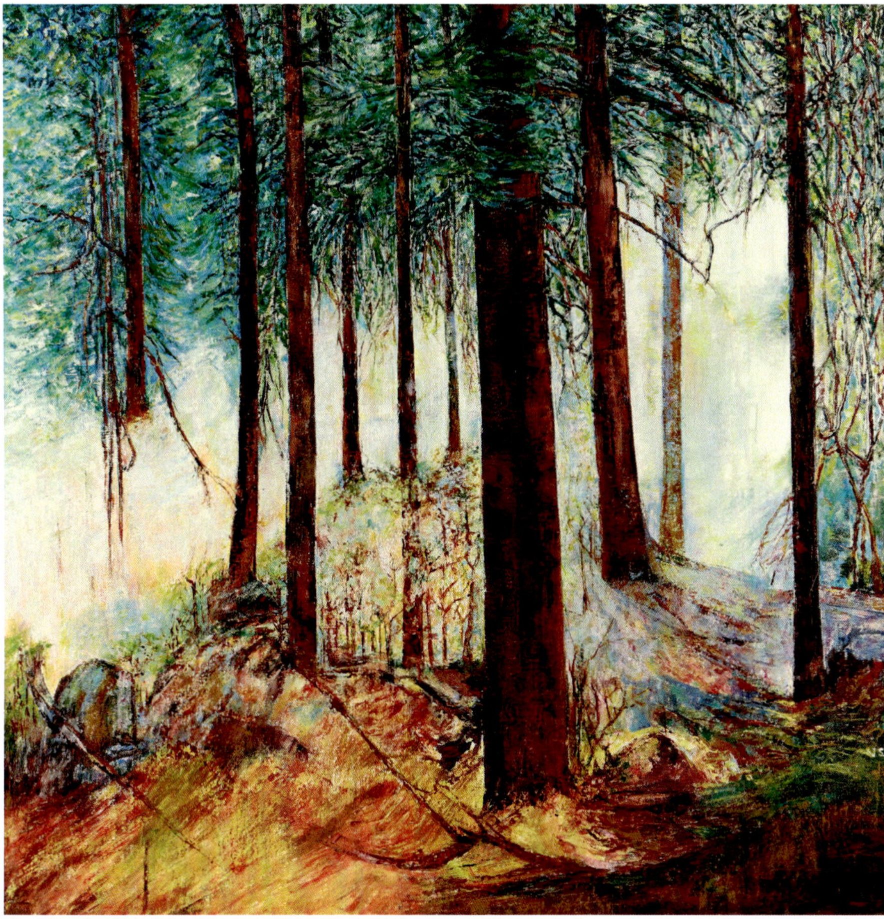

Little Green is Left

32"x32" • Oil on Canvas

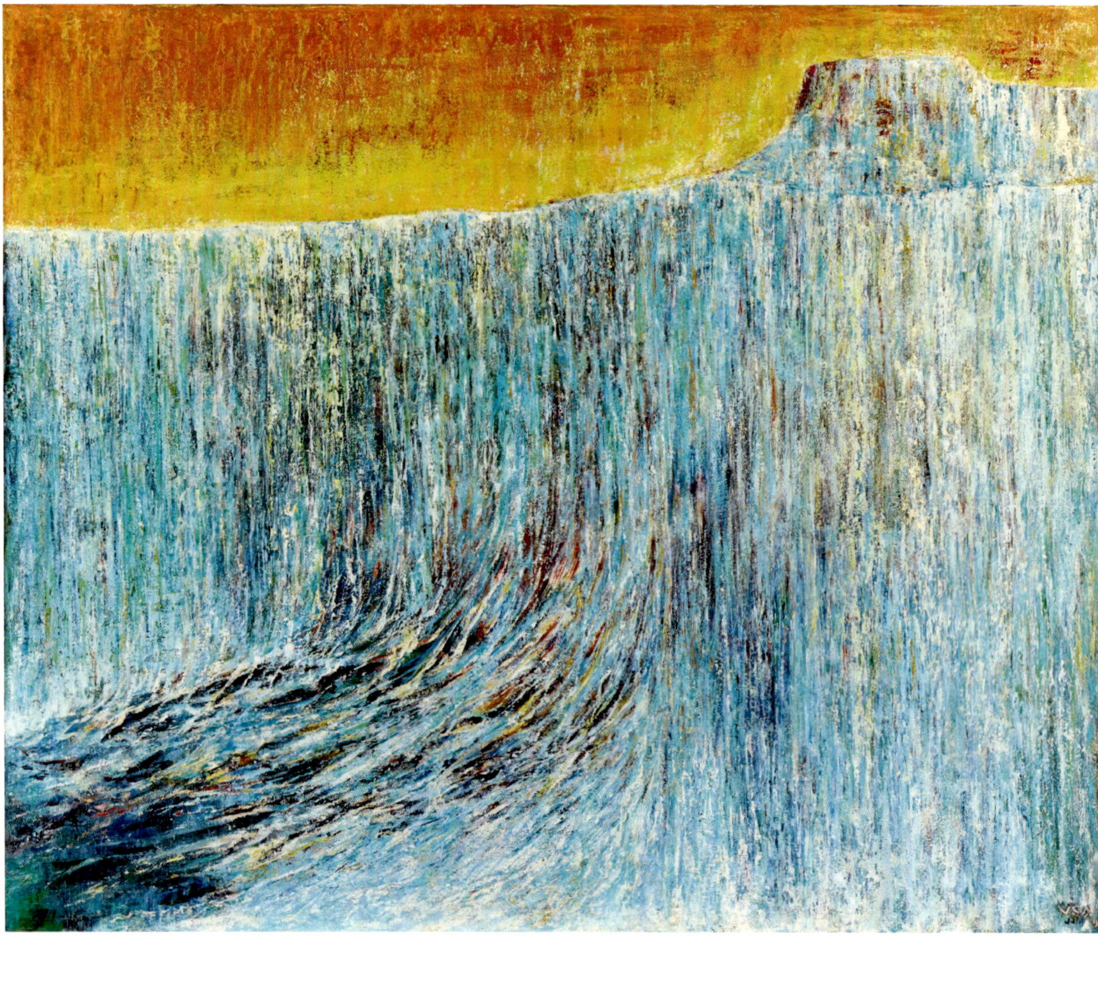

Underground Waterfall

32"x40" • Oil on Canvas

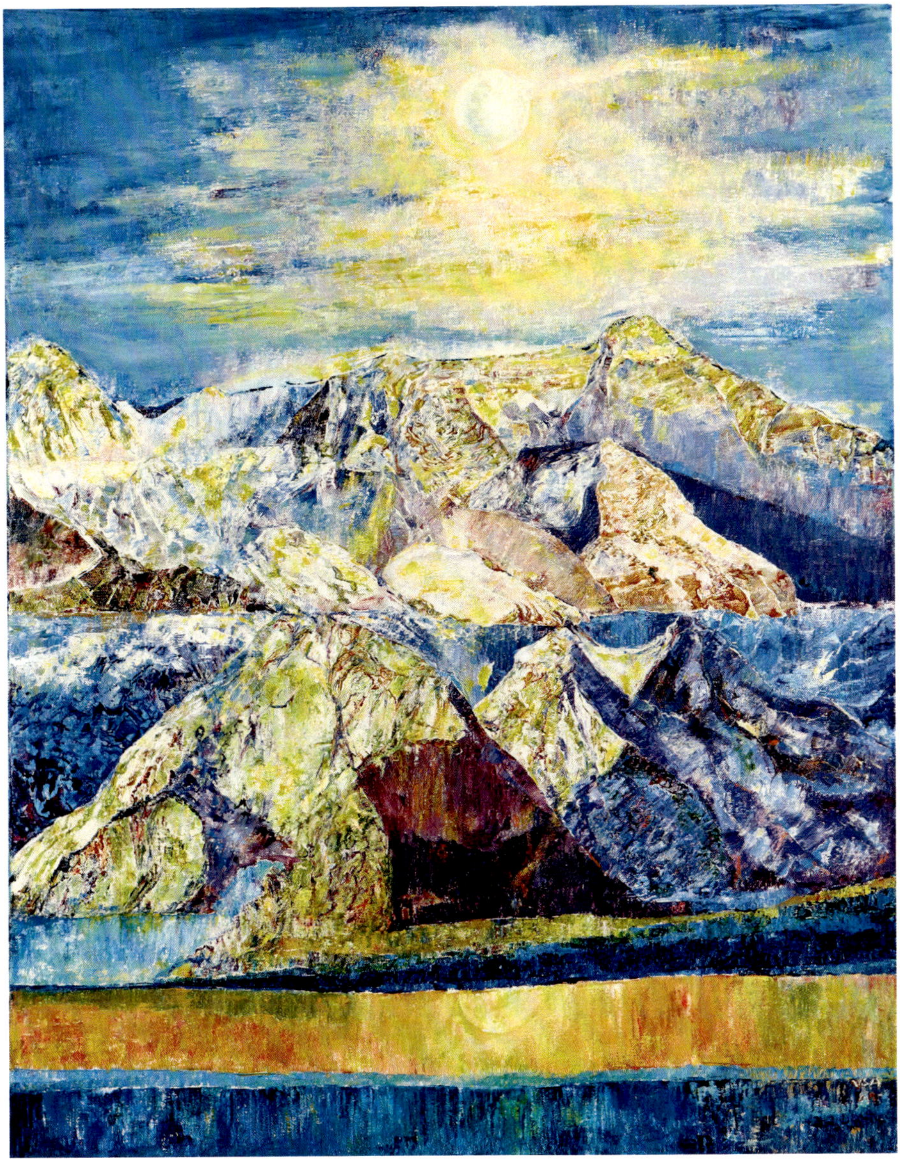

Moon and the Mountain

24”x30” • Oil on Canvas

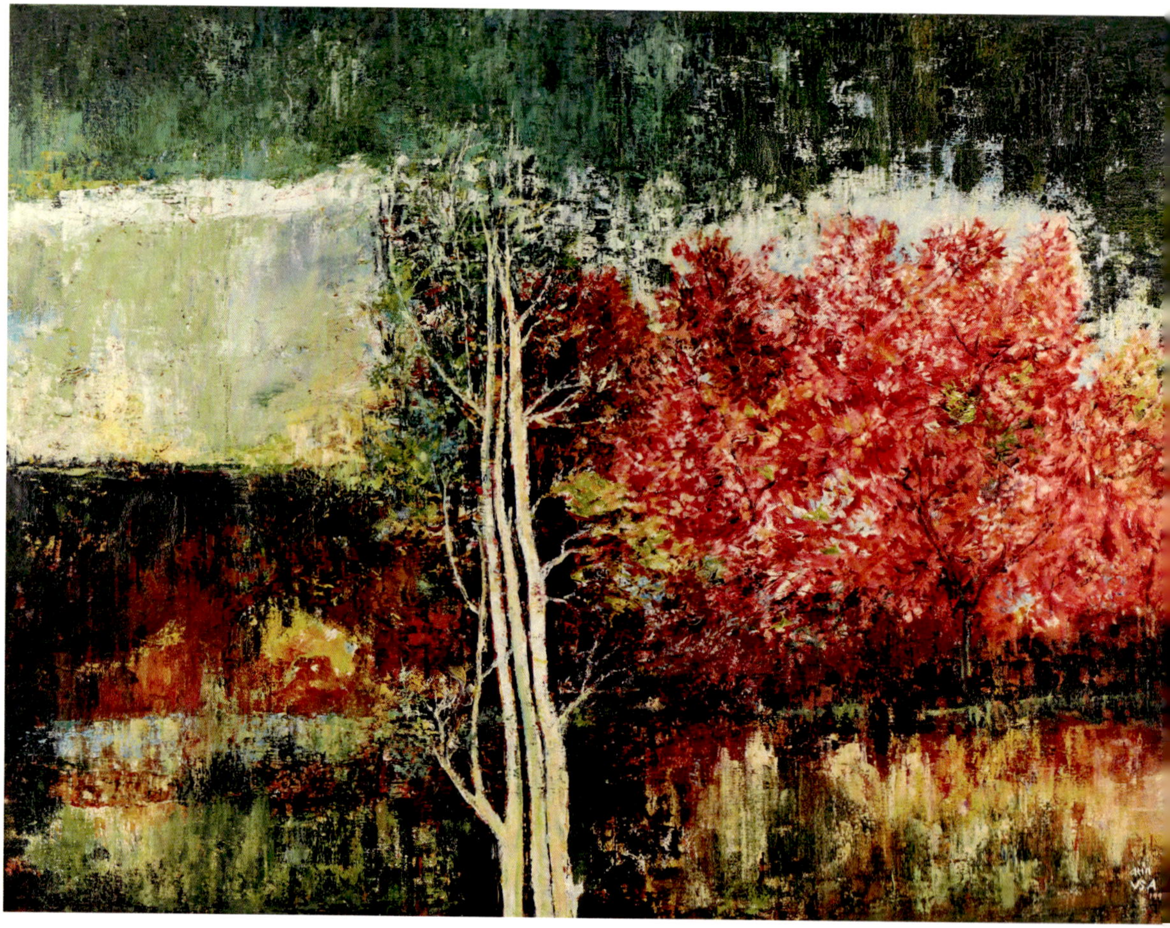

Landscape

40”x36” • Oil on Canvas

have survived on the walls in Caves No.IX and X, belong to the 5th and 6th centuries. Ajanta paintings attracted the attention of scholars when they were accidentally discovered by a British hunter in 1843. James Fergusson gave it the due publicity it deserved. The art of the Ajanta wall paintings indicate a long process of evolution. The realistic trends in fragments found in the old paintings resemble the sculptural carvings on the entrance gates of Sanchi and Bagh *stupas* of the 2nd and 1st century BC.

Vishnudharmottara Purana, a treatise on art of painting and sculpture of Indian classical period, had dealt with ideals and directive principles for ancient Indian paintings and sculptures. The technique and method of representation of Ajanta frescos are based on the six elements (Shadāngas) prescribed in the above mentioned Purana. They are:-

(i) Rupabheda – Differentiation of Forms

(ii) Pramana – Proportion

(iii) Bhāva – Expression of Emotions

(iv) Lavanya Yojana – Depiction of Charm

(v) Sadrisha – Faithful to Life

(vi) Varnika Bhanga – Blending of Colours

Buddhist monks excavated the caves and developed the surfaces of walls for painting the frescos. They completed the paintings to the standard of perfection as works of art.

Those artist-monks were devoted to meditation and cultivation of a higher life. Unity of purpose and completeness of finish were unrivalled elsewhere in the 6th century wall paintings. The artists of Ajanta thoroughly understood the principles of decorative art in their highest and noblest sense.

The Government of India during colonial rule sanctioned annual grants for the purpose of making life-size copies of Ajanta frescos on canvas. The students and teachers of Sir J.J. School of Art, were engaged in this work, which was completed during the years 1872-1885.

Mr. Griffiths, ex-Dean of Sir J.J. School of Art, writes in his book on Ajanta Art – "The most curious and interesting phase of my Indian experience was the initiation of Hindu, Parsi and Goanese students in the mysteries of an art still congenial to the oriental temperament and hand. After some practice peculiarities of handling and treatment grew to be second nature of these artists and I am persuaded to think that no European, no matter how skilful, could have so completely caught the spirit of the originals. The decorative work of J.J. School of Art and practice of original design were greatly influenced by this work. It was a great source of inspiration for Indian artists."

The basic aim of the art of Ajanta was to edify Buddhism. But there is nothing spiritual in painting stories on the previous lives of Buddha. Characters depicted in the frescos are free from the mysteries of life and metaphysical speculations. The painters of Ajanta unfold a grand human drama in which participants are not Gods but princes, sages, heroes, men and women belonging to different walks of life. The joy which emanated from this essentially human approach to art with men and women, in strength and liveliness of animals, in rhythmic steps of dancers and musicians, and in the joyous participation of people watching through their windows of houses and streets to witness the Royal processions, is symbolic in unity of mankind. The work of Ajanta cave paintings is accomplished in execution, consistent in conventions, vivacious and varied in design and full of such evident delight in beautiful forms and colours is social in content and religious in execution. The art appreciator cannot help ranking it with the art of the highest quality in the ancient world. This style of painting was also prevalent in Nepal, Tibet, Afghanistan and neighbouring oriental countries.

With the passage of time the subjects and styles of painting gradually shifted towards religion with the consequent stress on iconography and *Puranic* legends. The Sanchi and Baharut *stupa* stone carvings resemble the style and technique of ivory carvers. It means that the carvers were not well versed in the technique of cutting figures in stone. Figurative compositions of stone carvers made a remarkable progress in Gupta-Vakataka dynastic period. A classic example is the 8th century Kailasanath temple of Ellora, the first of its kind in the history of world sculpture. This entire temple was excavated and carved out, in three stages, from top to bottom, from a single rock. Deep relief carving on the outside wall panels are almost three dimensional in effect. The exquisite figures depicting *Puranic* stories seem to subtly change expressions with the play of light, and come out alive before the beholder. This is only the beginning of India's legends in stone sculpture.

Beauty and serenity of figurative sculptures and decorative carvings of ancient monumental temples of India, with their stylistic differences in different regions, are an experience to be cherished and not described in words. It may not be an exaggeration to say that mega-structures of modern times, based on science and technology, may fail to give as much joy and ecstasy compared to those marvelous structures and temples with their creative stone carvings of the wonder that was ancient India.

Vishnudharmottaram and *Bharatnatyashastra*, ancient treatise on fine arts, had prescribed the principles and guidelines to depict rhythmic and graceful movements of human figures in sculptural carvings on the outside walls of temples in India. Visuals of different iconic images with their symbols were worked out by saints and visionaries. Sculptors were trained in the guilds of artists and selected for particular types of works after elaborate practice and training. Distortions in lines and figures were considered as bad in taste and lacking in competence of the artist. But in Modern Art, distortion is accepted as a necessary element to express the characteristics of the artist and his personality. Art ideals change depending on the changing cultures of emerging societies and their trends.

During the British colonial rule in India, many Western scholars including Professor Griffiths of Sir J.J. School of Art, Bombay, Professor Percy Brown of Calcutta School of Art, Mrs. Stella Kramrish from America and Mr. Basham from Australia studied systematically varied aspects of ancient Indian temples and their characteristic elements of beauty in temple-structures, sculptures and paintings. Dr. Moti Chandra has also examined the styles and techniques of early Indian paintings of Ajanta and Bagh frescos, and later developments of painting on religious book-covers and illustrations of mediaeval period. With the spread of knowledge and exchange of ideas, American and European nations recognised the aesthetic values of the priceless treasures of traditional Indian artifacts, including iconographic stone statues, bronzes, decorative metal works and miniatures. Art lovers and collectors from all over the world have acquired during the last century, India's most beautiful traditional art and craft works, with or without Indian Government's permission.

Name and fame of Indian artists were not considered important in acquisition of these unique and beautiful art works of India.

American sculptor, Carmel Berkson who came to India in 1970 and settled in India in 1977 for study and practice of Indian sculpture is the author of five books. She said, "India has great culture and I saw the aesthetic sensibility and brilliance in ancient Indian sculpture. I gave up my practice as I felt like I know nothing. I do not understand why modern Indian sculptors look to the west for inspiration". A Padma Shri award winner Berkson opined further, "Great sculptors of the temples of Ellora, Mahabalipuram, Halebid-Bellur did not put their names on their works as they did not have any ego."

The great art of ancient India was produced by trained groups of artists and sculptors who were not inspired by any commercial ambitions. Those artists were moved by missionary zeal to create classic sculptures of iconic significance with a devotion to work as worship. The traditional ancient Indian art was governed by certain principles and rules of aesthetic significance to showcase rhythm and unity in diversity, as eternal truth.

Abstract Art and its Religious Source in India

The artifacts from the Indus Valley culture convey in no uncertain terms the meaning and significance of the ancient Indian art forms. Their art was conceptual from the very beginning of civilisation. Tiny seals expertly carved in relief, and the red sandstone torso, measuring a mere 4½", depicts the power of expression of line and form irrespective of their small sizes. Image of the Indus Bull carved on a 3 sq.cm seal when projected on the screen is transformed as if magically, into a powerful bull of massive strength. This memory image is stylised and does not appear to be of a particular bull but represents the generalised character of that animal. The torso of Harappa reveals the form and function of human body with the inherent *prana* which manifests in the convex bulge of the limbs of human body. One can see continuation of this conceptual art forms in India even after 2 millennium years. During the Kushana period in 1st century A.D. elements of Greco-Roman art were introduced for the first time in Indian sculpture. But the tubular forms of human body as seen in the Bhaja carvings, and engraved metal bowls of that period, are obvious examples of persistence of conceptual art forms of earlier genre.

Indian tradition has attached great significance to the life and living of people. It has always sought to develop a complete growth of human personality through its art and philosophy. There are many attempts by the ancient Indian thinkers at revitalisation of concepts and forms in visual art. We have ample proof of this aspect in the treatise of early classical period such as Vishnudharmottaram, Kamasutra, and many other ancient documents containing art concepts of ancient Indians. A thorough discussion on aesthetic forms and content, style and technique for perfect rendering of paintings, symbolism and iconography for divine ideals etc., is to be found in the early documentation. Significance of art for spiritual growth and positive personality and its relation to the Indian philosophy is made obvious in the material culture of the people.

The 20th century Suprematist concept of pure form for the expression of supreme or divine feeling in visual art was not new to ancient Indians. Although during the Kushana period the Greco-Roman ideals of divine beings founded solely by contemplation of human form (anthropomorphic) was introduced for the first time in India against the doctrine of Hinayana, the Indian thinking on the subject is clear from the writings of Shukracharya. He says that the artists should attain the images of Gods by means of spiritual contemplation only. The spiritual vision is the best and trusted standard for the artists. He should not depend upon the visible objects perceived by external senses. From the literature and artifacts of Indian classical period it is explicit that art cannot be reduced to mere rules of logic and technique, anatomy or perspective, style or fashion so that the creative faculty on which vitality of all art depends is drowned in empty formularies of intellectual, moral and aesthetic value. We invariably find that the classical art of India is abstract and the quality of surface realism is subordinated to the ideas of abstract beauty. In this art one sees the overall efforts of the Indian artist to knit together the inner meaning and outer form like thought and speech as poet Kalidas has put it.

The Greek philosopher Plato had said that geometrical forms are the most beautiful as they are the essential and purest forms in nature. This idea has been carried forward by the 20th century artist Cezannc through his paintings and later on it manifested in the Cubism of Picasso and Braque. Many later 'isms' of Western art namely Suprematism, Constructivism, Neo-Plasticism and Abstract Art were the logical consequences of this single great thought of Plato. But the Hindu iconographic art of ancient India like the modern Western art movements, referred to above, joins geometry with aesthetics. An equilateral triangle is a geometric symbol of the three coordinated cosmic powers, namely, (i) will (ii) knowledge and (iii) action, -three aspects of one divine form. The stable triangle ▲ = male principle and unstable triangle ▼ = female principle embrace to form the first act of creation a star ★ or six petalled lotus symbol of mystic divine embrace. *Yantra* and *Mantra* symbolising pure form and pure sound were considered to be emanating from the divine world which set the universe in motion. *Vishnudharmottaram*, therefore, refers to the art of music, dance and imagery as the different expressions of the universal rhythm. We may, therefore, conclude that the Indian artists have been dealing with profound metaphysical ideas which were considered as outside the limit of art by the West. The Chola bronze 'Nataraj' is a classic example of Indian iconographic statue of cosmic being.

As the ancients deliberately chose imaginative rather than naturalistic ideals of divine form, symbolism became the most significant element in their visual expression. Symbols in Indian religious art are expressions of man's search of God. These expressions are vivid, instantaneous revelation of the mysterious. Although Indian artists were not ascetics who shut themselves out of the world, they were mystics who communed with nature to find the secrets of the universal life. That the art was practiced for spiritual growth and flowering of human personality is again evident from an early treatise which states, "Painting cleans the mind and curbs anxiety, augments future good, causes the greatest delight, kills the evils of bad dreams and pleases the household deity. Painting is also the best of all arts and conducive to Dharma i.e. right conduct."

Indian religious art is closely linked to mysticism in India. Mysticism has its fount in the content of religion and it had also been the inspiration of oriental philosophy, poetry, art and music. The mystical element enters into religious experience of a devotee when the religious feelings explore the consciousness of the beyond, i.e. of an unseen over and above the seen. This results when the non-rational unconscious elements predominate and determine the emotional life and intellectual attitude. Thus there is an extension of normal consciousness, a release of latent powers and a widening of vision which brings in a direct experience of the presence of the omnipotent. This personal experience is fully and absolutely valid to those who have inner yearning to see the unseen and seek the divine. The ancient Indian sculptors under the guidance of saints and visionaries aimed to expand the qualities of their mind and vision by creating abstract images of their Gods. These images, symbolic and abstract, were the result of contemplation on metaphysical elements. Metamorphosis and metaphysics had been the best principle in the evolution of Indian divine ideals. *Ardhanarinateshwar* should be regarded as an early attempt in this direction.

My intension here is not to survey the Indian art history with reference to various significant works done in the past and modern times, but to point out the value attached to the practice of art in enhancement of spiritual life of the individual artist and the society. The aim and purpose of true Indian art was to serve humanity by influencing one's own spiritual life. In other words, to enhance *paradharma* through the enhancement of *swadharma*. Havell made this point clear when he wrote, "Indian art is not concerned with conscious striving after beauty as a thing worthy of seeking after for its own sake; its main endeavour is always directed towards the realisation of an idea reaching through the finite to the infinite. The central idea of Indian art is that beauty is inherent in spirit and not in matter. True aim of the Indian artist is not to extract beauty from nature but to reveal the life within life." The greatness of Indian art, like Indian philosophy, lies in its aim and practice for enhancement of life on this planet. In this context I may safely surmise that the true Indian art of the past and present is essentially mystical in nature and the artists practicing it are bound to grow spiritually in stature within their lifetime. The world famous sculptors of modern era like Brancusi and Arp were so influenced by the oriental philosophy that in their sculptures they tried to seek and reveal the life pulsating throughout our universe.

The question that confronts us today is whether Indian art and artists of this century have the same aim and purpose in life, i.e. to lead humanity to a blissful life of spiritual growth, peace and harmony? This question is a poser to all the successful artists of today for introspection. No doubt this is a most challenging task for the Indian artist of today, when he has to confront commercialism and competition for his material success. But material success can never be an indicator to success in creative activity.

On the contrary it is likely to upset the balance by boosting one's ego and thus misleading him in the spiritual path of creative activity. It may however be observed that the art teachers and artists who are on the periphery of creative art contribute immensely to the development of pure art.

Art always changes like a river changing its course depending upon the environment but the continual flow is never broken. Indian art has also changed in this century accepting many new directions, art ideas and visual stimulants, but like the river Ganga, Indian art has also not lost its mysterious and religious depth. Every true Indian Modern artist is by nature a creative philosopher seeking advancement in his spiritual life by practice of his own skills with which he is gifted. Modern Indian art should not therefore be seen as a modification and manipulation of art forms of the past but a reincarnation of new forms born out of man's quest for spiritual growth. Such art would pour from, what I may term as the mystic state of the mind which experiences what is beyond the ordinary vision. Acharya Rajnish said that to achieve such a state of mind the artist should first empty his heart and become a flute, a hollow bamboo, through which the universe sings divine music. The great universal flood comes only when the artist is so humble, that he is almost nobody. Kandinsky, the Russian born 20th century artist, has influenced Western Modern Art through his 'improvisations' (i.e. practice of painting without conscious and planned approach to the canvas) and his treaties on colour and spiritual art is not new to the Indian aesthetics. Also, it may be pointed out that the source of aesthetic theory accepted by Paul Klee is Indian in origin. To an Indian born artist who has a natural bent for philosophic approach to the problem of life, abstractions in art is not new as it was to the early 20th century artist of European countries. It would therefore be wrong to presume that the modern Indian art is the result of the influence from the West. Indian artists of modern times seem to be trailing behind due to lack of competitive spirit and robust aggression. But true Indian artists, though small in number, are and will be creating new art forms which shall be conducive to the future good of the world and humanity. This art will be free from pseudo art practiced for commercial gains and competitive success. This art shall positively light the path of creative spirit. There shall be no encounters or East and West confrontations in this kind

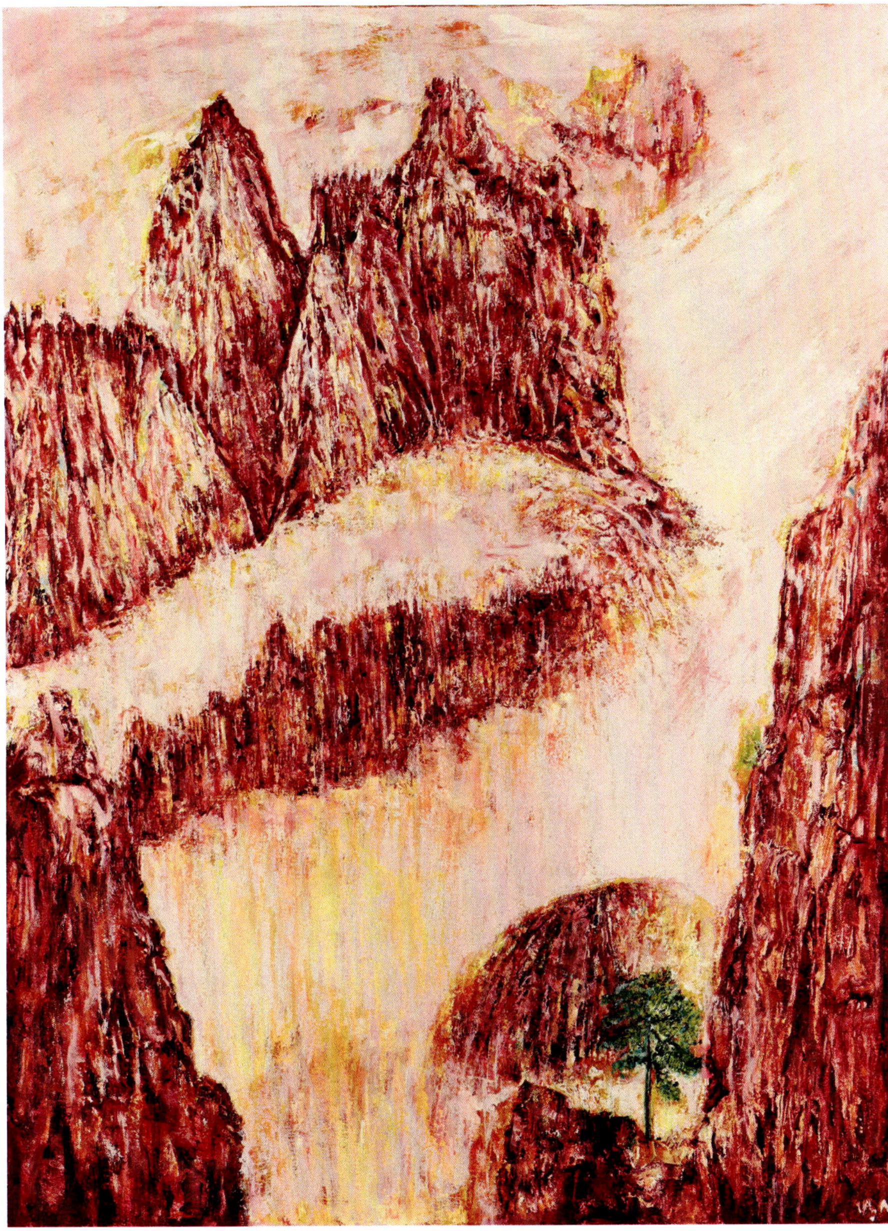

Mountains

24”x30” • Oil on Canvas

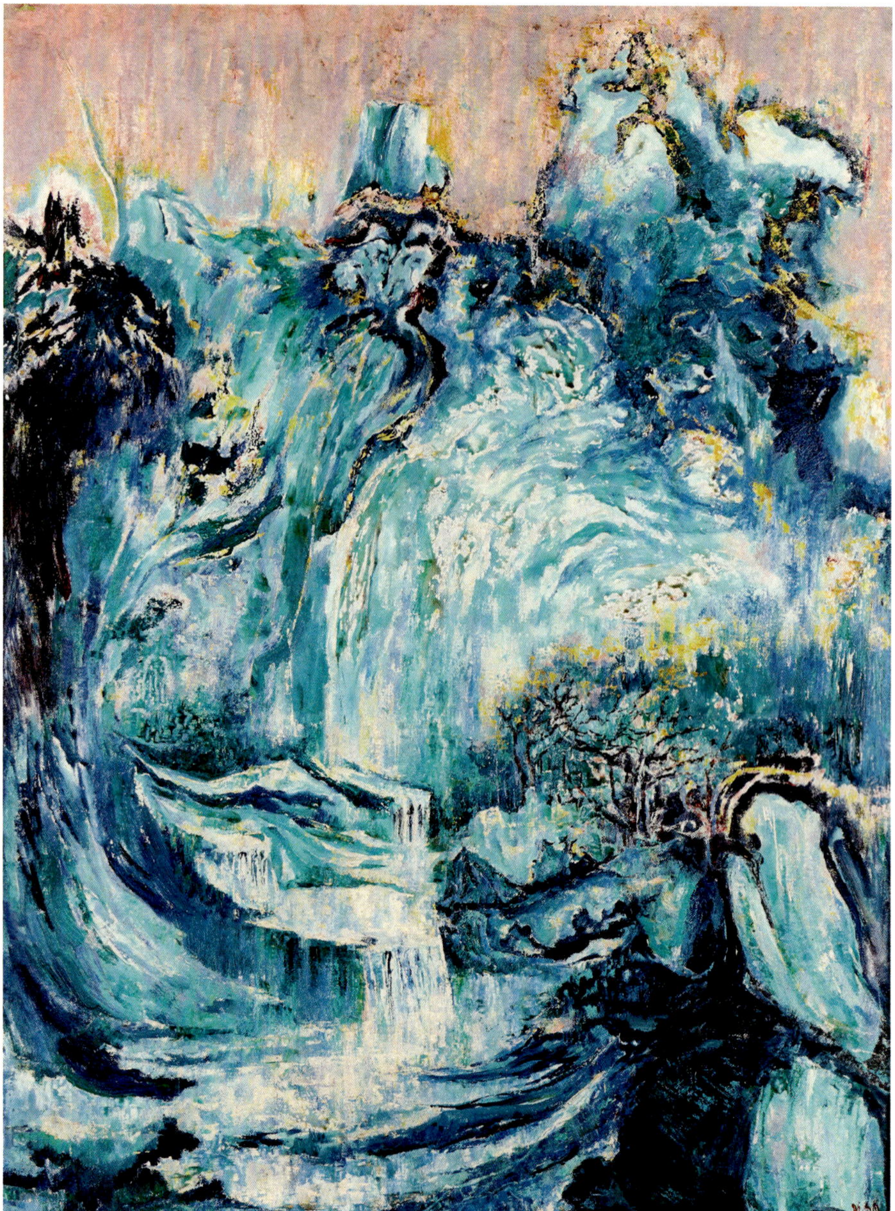

Landscape

24”x30” • Oil on Canvas

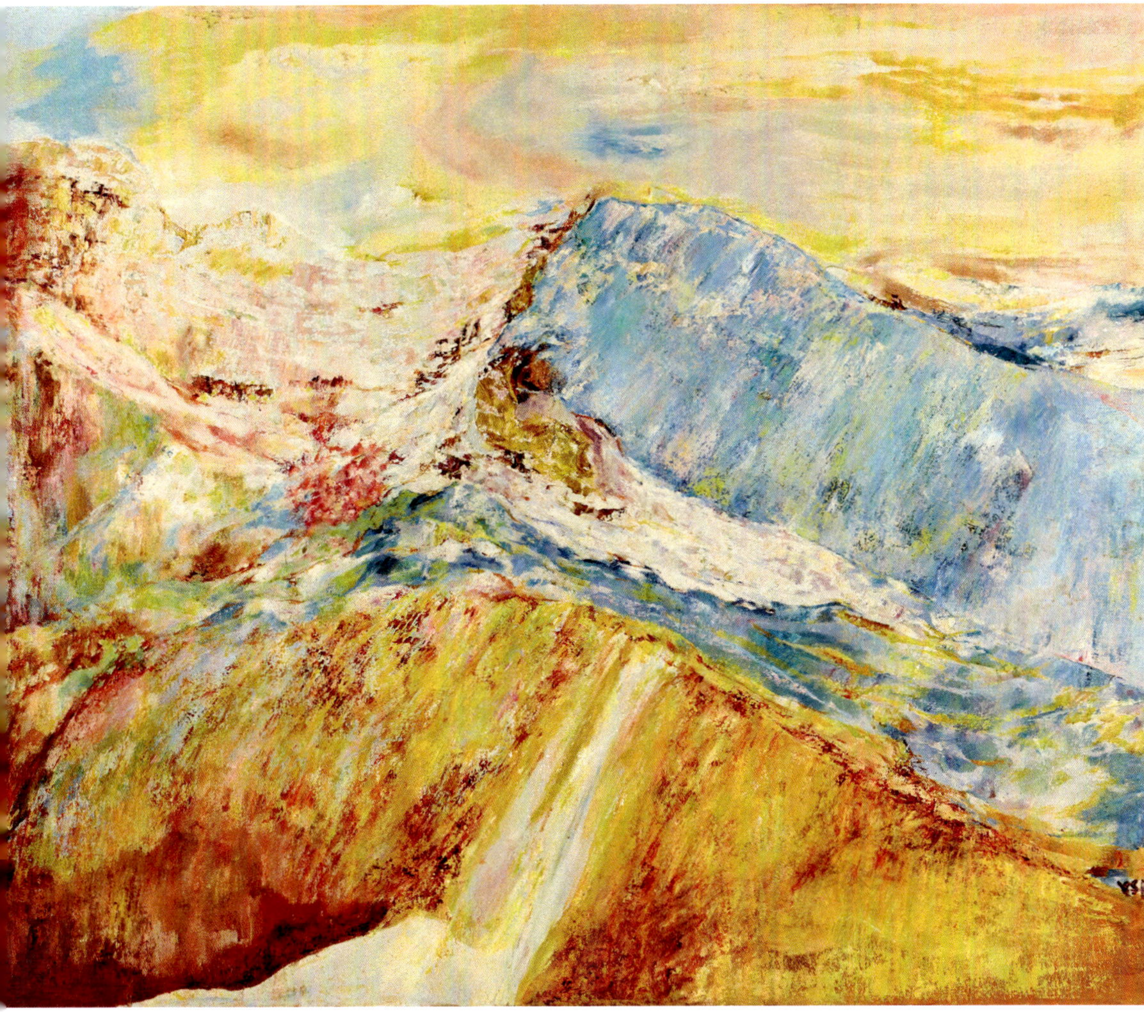

Mountain - Nilgiri

40”x36” • Oil on Canvas

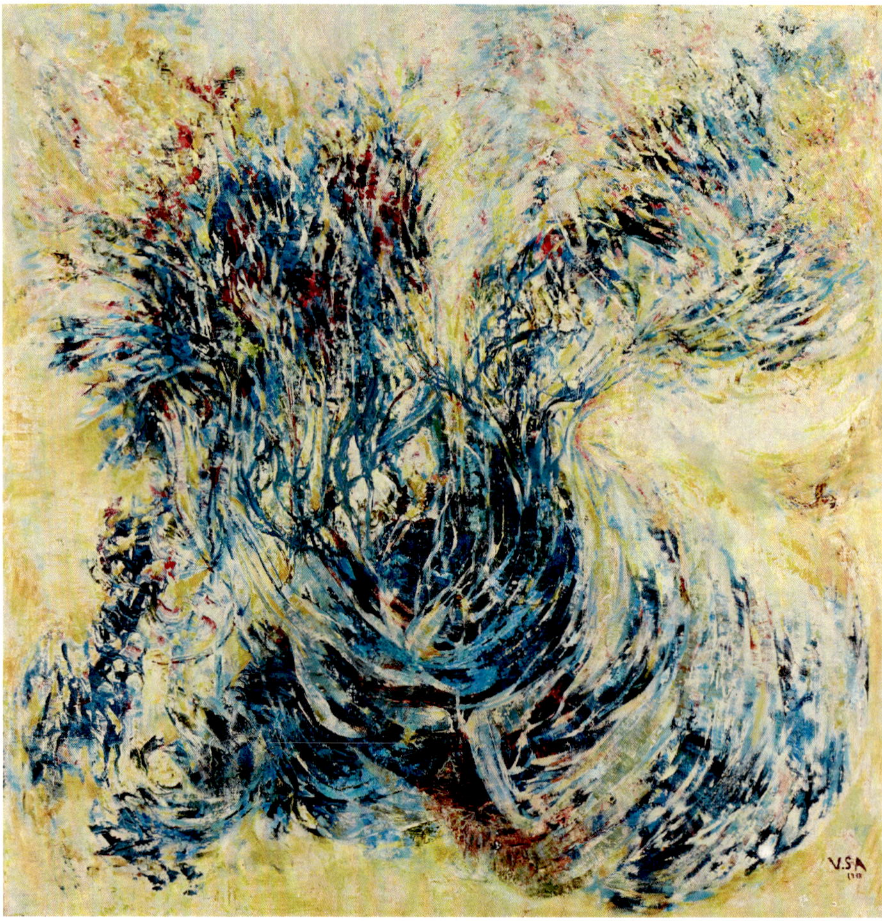

Vibration and Creation

33"x33" • Oil on Canvas

of art. It will be a new vision of harmonious order for the future of mankind. Such work shall emerge from the spiritual and mystical paths, from the faith and total surrender to the highest power. Indian sculptors and painters with such religious faith and fervour added a glorious chapter to the art of India in the past. Modern Indian artists too having a religious attitude towards their own creative ability will not fail in their mission.

PART II

INTROSPECTION

'ART is not Anybody's Business'

Choosing paintings and sculptures of outstanding merits is often problematic for art critics and appreciators because there is no definite or fixed standard for judging the excellence of art works. Arbitrary selection based on individual tastes or likes and dislikes, is not conductive to reliable judgment for great works of contemporary Modern Art. The general tendency of accepting the distinguished artist's works as quality art works, is also wrong because the success of such artists may be due to his lasting influence on the art market and art politics.

A sound judgment for promoting or choosing fine art works of outstanding quality is possible only by a process of imaginative contemplation. Contemplation without adequate knowledge of the artist's concepts of abstraction in his art is likely to reveal only superficial and surface appeal of the art work. The pulsating life of a remarkable art work of purely abstract nature can be conceived only when several aspects, including the artist's emotions, inspirations and the process of creations, become familiar to the percipient. Contemplation is the only way to penetrate visual art by visual sense to reach its soul.

Even the art that apparently has no immediate message but is created spontaneously in a joyous mood, will lift up the spectator and take him out of himself to give him temporary release from trouble and worry and refresh his mind, if he can contemplate for a while. Thus visual art can serve all those who stand and look with an open mind to grasp the harmony, rhythm and joy emanating from forms and colours of a painting.

Interpreting art works by means of words can be very difficult for both the writer and reader. Painters choose to paint rather than write because no written description and analysis of the simplest picture can be a complete substitute for it. Often ideas expressed in visual arts defy translation into another form. Visual art needs to be interpreted and enjoyed visually.

In our century of science and technology there is no consistency of styles and techniques. The art world is aware that Modern Art of this century is very much influenced by modern philosophy of change and evolution. Modern trend is that of world civilisation. The revolutionary changes of modern world on all fronts including socio-political, economic and cultural have given a characteristic temper to this century. The traditional institutions and values have changed and are changing. Groups of traditional artists have lost their significance. The fine artist of our century is free and independent to create his own art. He can also proclaim that 'Art is for Art's sake'. He can use his gift as a surplus given to him by God or Nature for development of his own personality. The artist's creative imagination can lead him to his spiritual energy which seeks its outlet in creations. His perceptual forces are its potent factors. The world becomes completely his own when it comes within the range of his emotions. This world becomes a part of the artist's personality with his love and hatred, pleasure and pain, fear and wonder continually working upon him. The creative activities of such artists who are not influenced by the money market, remain distinct and should not be labelled as a profession. Pure art is the result of a dynamic form of mediation and contemplation. Applied art, also known as commercial art, is a profession. It helps to develop and promote products and services of everyday use through illustrations, photographs and many other visual aids. In a world of money market, applied art and industry go hand in hand for fashionable creations. Fine art is practiced for its own sake and is free from market influence. Delight of the artist is the award of his creation. Exhibition of his works is a festival and celebration of joy for society.

In ancient India practice of fine art for its own sake was encouraged. It was believed that the daily practice of painting develops the spiritual life and personality of its devotee. The main function of Art is to unite the cultural world.

Art and Science are Poles Apart

Science is a discipline to discover and use abstract forces for the benefit of mankind and also save the world against the tyranny of adverse conditions on this planet. Abstract forces of science and its creations have neither emotions nor feelings of mutual love. Scientists created monstrous war machines and weapons like atom bombs, which can destroy this world. Science can produce computers and robots to serve, but not men and women of feelings who can give and take the joy of life. Unlike forces of science, art with its fund of emotions, love and joy can unite this world and make this very earth a heaven for everyone to celebrate the joy of living. The forces of art cannot destroy, except the bad and ugly. It is nature's gift to realise the secret of our existence and celebrate the unity of eternal life and its consciousness on the living planet. In other words, art's pursuit is to make the whole world a family, with a bond of beauty, security and love.

In the modern world of anxiety and fear, terrorism and its repercussions, expectations and disappointments, technological creations of television and their various channels of entertainment cannot lift a sensitive person from the frustrations and drudgery of life. People all over the world are now adopting the ancient Indian practice of yoga and contemplation for betterment of body and spirit. For a lasting cultural civilisation of the world, art and science need to go hand in hand, because, both emotions and intelligence are complementary and supplementary for man's survival and progress.

Appreciation and Evolution of Creative Visual Art

How do we distinguish between good art and bad art? There is no precise answer, and no answer would be right for all individuals all the time. It is subject to sensibility and maturity of the critical eye of the percipient. To start with, one can look for positive qualities perceivable in an art work by a contemplative process.

What does the painting or sculpture represent? Great subject does not mean creation of great art work because a beautiful painting does not depend upon a beautiful subject matter. Its subject may be factual or an analogy drawn from everyday experience of the visual world, or a statement of personal world of geometry, or the world of spirituality inspired by the inner vision of the artist. Art ideas, inspiration and contemplation for the creative process are more important than the subject matter for creation of great art.

What about skills and techniques? Skill in draughtsmanship, colour application or observation of light and shades, by itself, may not create good work of art although some great artists have employed super skills in their works. The required skill is born with the art and ideas of inspiration. Only skills do not guarantee any quality in the work of art. Success of art works depends upon the artist's desire to express his ideas and feelings powerfully and ingeniously so as to move the beholder with a forceful impact of the work.

Quality art works are and should be visuals of harmonious orchestration of colours and forms, balance and movements, textures and structures with designs of artist's creations to reveal the rhythm and unity in a masterpiece. In visual art vigorous brush work suggestive of depths and dimensions, convey the power and inspiration of good art works. Brushwork in paintings and handling of materials in sculptures must fulfill the artist's particular requirements of creation.

Achievements and success of artistic creations can be conceived only by enlightened visual perceptions.

Different groups of artists all over the world have tried to formulate their own rules for making works of art. These rules have helped to produce works of good calibre. But such rules are constantly being broken by restless artists and sometimes their new concepts and ideas have produced outstanding works of great interest. This proves that no rules can be considered as a permanent yardstick for judging great art work. The question therefore is whether qualitative judgments can be made about the works of art at all. It is only in the field of visual art that the opinions of enlightened art patrons and artists matter because their valuation is based on emotional contents and powerful aesthetic attraction of paintings and sculptures.

Contemporary artists of this century are bound to study characteristics and art ideas of different schools and styles of major artists of past centuries. They explore the internal and external influences that have made impact on the developments of contemporary art. It is therefore useful to consider the artist's attitudes towards the technical aspects of form, style, colour application and perspective etc. and also his philosophy of art and practices.

The value of the work of art depends on the artist's intention and quality of that intention and also his success at the technical realisation of that intention. Relative values of different artists and their arts cannot be compared because each artist has his own intention and he tries his best to express profound truths in his own particular way. The best and easy way to be familiar with an artist's intention is to discuss with the artist, if possible, or ask yourself relevant questions on the style and techniques of the artist, his compositions as well as colour concepts. Also try to see many paintings of that artist to distinguish his characteristic art personality.

It is not correct to judge the value of paintings from the success of the artist's marketing skills and sale of his paintings, nor is it wise to presume that the artist who has painted a large number of paintings is better than the one who is not so prolific in his creations. In the selection of art of excellence the buyers must learn to choose and sort out the real diamonds from the artificial or imitative presentations. Some people are attracted much more by visual arts than others, not to a particular kind of painting or sculpture but to all of them. They simply enjoy looking at them. Their emotional involvement is so strong that the visual arts are essential for them to get rid of their tensions and boredom of the mundane existence. It is this strong emotion, the driving force, that urges people to look at the art and choose the paintings and sculptures of their liking for their collection. If some people believe that a particular piece of art work brings good luck and prosperity to them it cannot be said that they are superstitious because both visible and invisible forces are working on us, directly or indirectly. This personal preference is a good thing both for the art and its collector. One can always give good reasons to justify one's choice.

The message in pictorial art can be very powerful. It is also a personal view of the artist. The reception of the visual message is immediate and it crosses barriers of language and literacy. It can exaggerate and persuade the beholder to believe in things that actually do not exist. Distortions and abuse of natural forms is the method employed for a strong impact. The artist's intentions and his responsibility to the society become obvious in some cases when he exhibits his works. When an ego-centric artist without any self-criticism and moralistic approach creates works which hurt the feelings of society, he hurts himself and his art works. Such irresponsible works of art also creates social unrest to discredit his art. Freedom of art practice and expression demands introspection on the part of the artist.

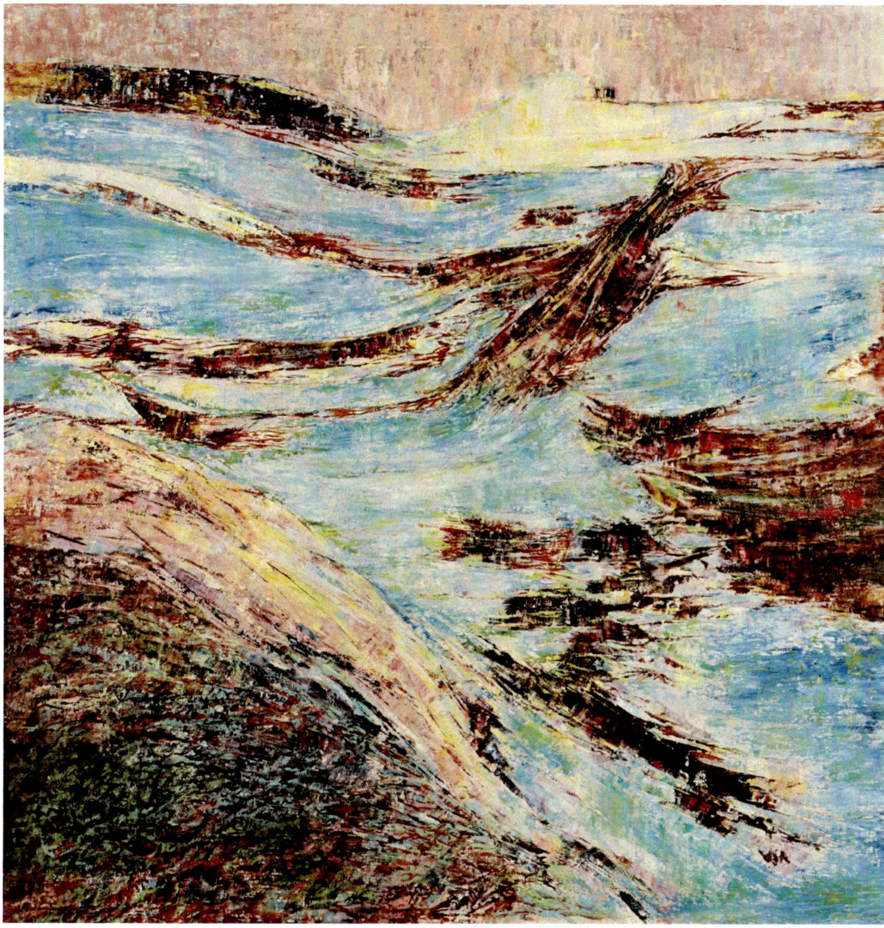

Confluence

33"x33" • Oil on Canvas

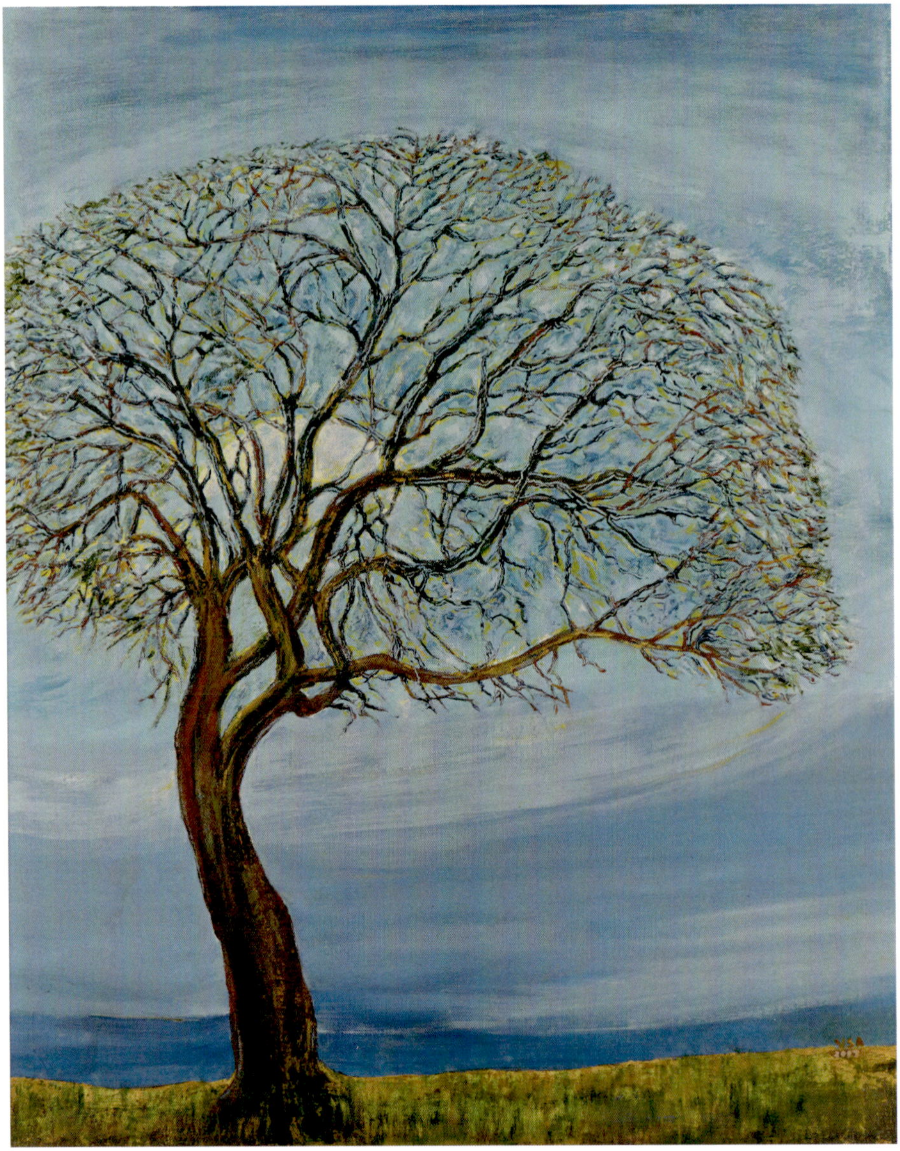

The Tree

24"x32" • Oil on Canvas

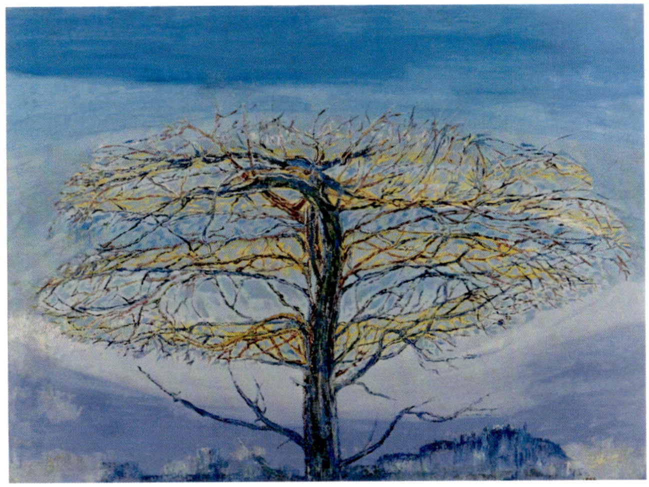

The Tree

32”x24” • Oil on Canvas

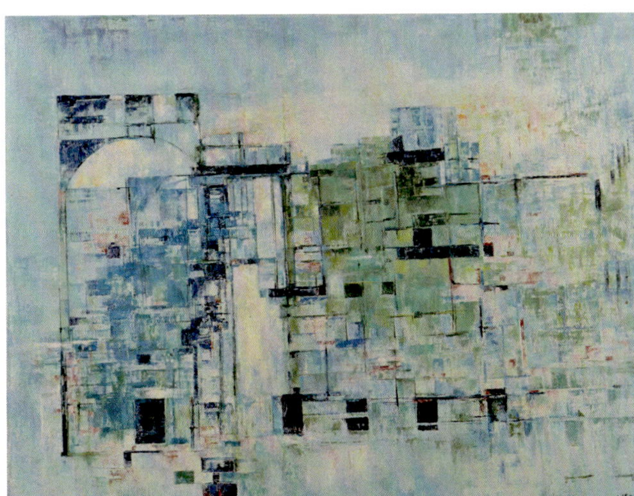

Colour Constructs

32”x24” • Oil on Canvas

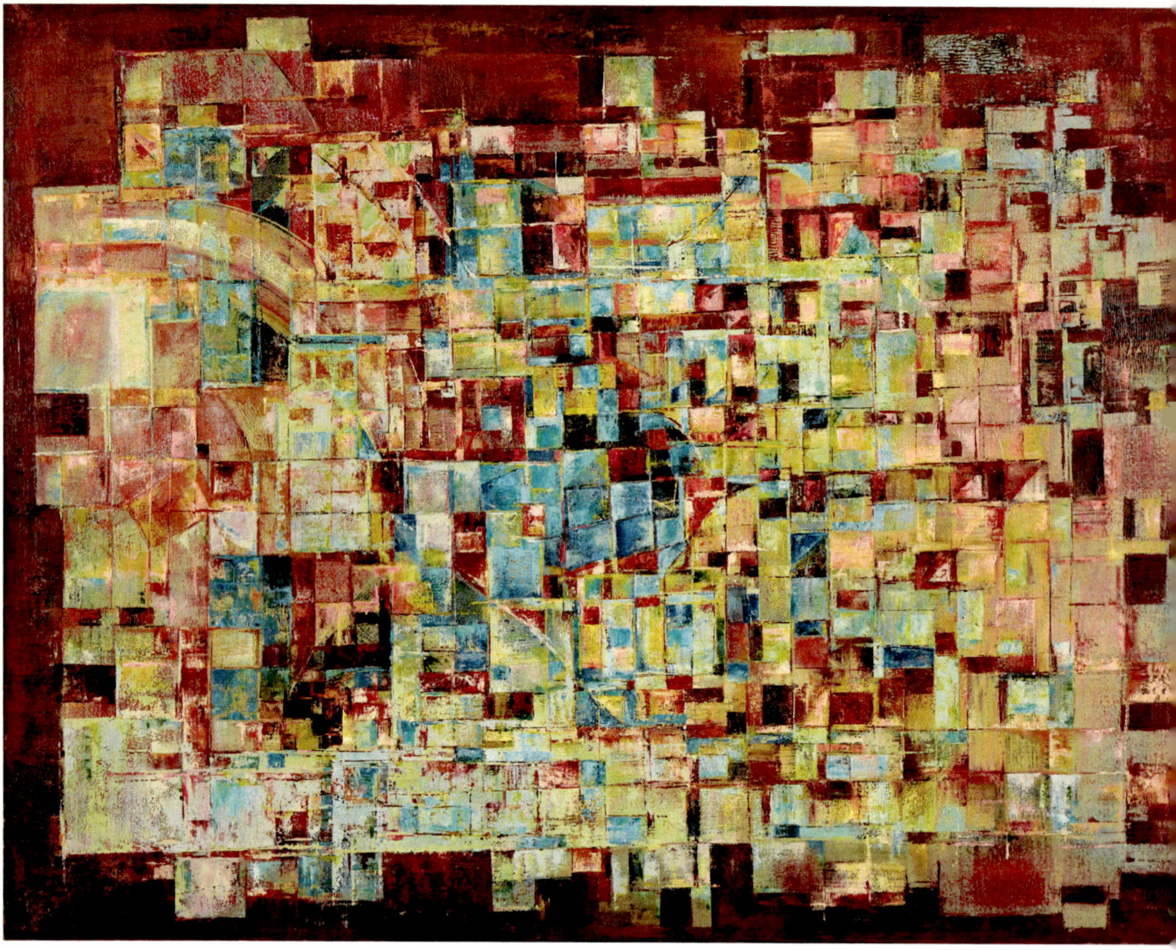

Colour Constructs

40”x36” • Oil on Canvas

PART III

MYSELF AND MY ART

"I think the principle of art is the principle of unity"

In art, the artist reveals himself and not his objects of knowledge. His knowledge from books is concealed in himself and his books. His mere information does not reveal him.

Every person has the right to select what he wants as a person, and this organic person has inherent powers to select from his surroundings in order to make them his own. He has his forces of attraction and repulsion by which he creates himself. The principal creative forces which transmute things in our living structure are our emotional forces. Our strong feelings for things we believe and like give us the inspiration for creative activities. Intensity of feeling for the divine makes us religious and creative. Mere knowledge of the divine cannot manifest our essence without the emotional fire.

I would like to try to find out the contents of the artist and his personality and how they are related to the outer world. To my mind and sense, the world appears as an individual and not merely a bundle of individual forces. This apparent world is our world. It has taken its special features of shape, colour and movement from the range and qualities of our perceptions. Apart from physical and chemical forces, man's perceptual forces are its potent factors. It is therefore a man's world and not the abstract world of physics and metaphysics. It becomes completely our own when it comes within the range of our emotions. This world with its seasonal changes excites our emotional activities and becomes a more intimate world of sentiments. It brings to us ideas, vitalised by feelings, to make the life-stuff of our nature. Descriptions of the beauty of sunrise and sunset, blossoming of trees in spring time, and falling of seasonal rains have perennial interest to us and we welcome them with our heartfelt love and pleasure. We feel it, because, by feeling it, we feel ourselves. This world and its environments are personal to the artist and they intensify his consciousness. On the other hand the world of science is the world of knowledge of abstract forces. We cannot touch it with our feelings and the elements of art personality. Artist Picasso once said, those who like a rose flower, should enjoy the fragrance and beauty of it. They should not bother about its chemistry. Facts of science and knowledge are different from the personal facts and feelings of the artist and his personality.

A landscape or a treescape by an artist is a personal expression of the artist and his love for the natural world -- his world and our world. It is a question of his personality and essence of expression of art and not a mirror image of nature. The truth about art is that no analytical treatment will help us in discovering the vital point in art. The true principle of art is the principle of unity. An artist's personality is an organic complex of matter and manner, thoughts and things, motives and actions, all rolled in one harmonious whole, with the forces of emotions and feelings. It grows with his growth and changes with his change.

The perceptions of the world are nourished from early childhood and one's surroundings. I think infantile attachments are, as a matter of fact, responsible in giving directions to our emotional growth. It may not, therefore, be out of place here to recollect and review my early childhood spent in the village of my birth.

I was born and brought up in a small village named Avarsa in the Karwar district of ex-Bombay Province. Our farm house was covered by thick forest and surrounded by beautiful mountain ranges of different hues and colours suggesting the magic of nature. There were no major or minor roads in the village of my birth. There were only bullock cart tracks and lanes. Walking in those streets, covered by tall trees with flowers and fruits, was not only challenging but thrilling for a six year old boy like me. I always walked in the company of other boys because many a time unexpected things including reptiles were sighted in those lanes. At that age my keen sense of observation and powerful eyesight could recognise the objects of my interest even in remote corners of those streets. I think it was an opportune period for the development of my visual perceptions.

We lived in our farm house with an orchard of many varieties of mango trees. I had a natural attraction for trees. Swaying trees with their flowers and fruits were a joy for me to watch. In their movements of struggle and resistance against the monsoon winds the trees often dropped ripe mangos of different colours and varieties for me to choose. Mangoes are of many varieties unlike other fruits. They have different shapes, sizes, tastes, smells and colours. It was a pleasure to explore the smells, colours and tastes of different mangoes. I still remember our giant mango tree with small, round mangoes standing straight and tall, away from the rest of the trees. I personally liked that tree and always sat under its shelter. Whenever I wished for its fruits the tree would surprisingly drop one or two mangoes even when the wind was not blowing. It was my wish tree and also the speaking tree of my affection.

We know what life is neither by the outward features of things nor by the analysis of parts, but by our inner perception and sympathy. This is the real knowledge of an artist. The tree we see is separate from its surroundings. It struggles to maintain its creative individuality distinct from everything else in the universe. The more perfect the harmony with its world of the sun, soil and the seasons, the more perfect the tree becomes in its individuality. It is alone and positive in nature to maintain unity with the universe. In this unity is its fulfillment of existence. It is the first life on this planet. The second and third lives are those of animals and human beings.

"They also serve who only stand and wait", wrote the great poet John Milton, the author of the epic poems Paradise Lost and Paradise Regained. When I look at the standing trees, a graphic image of my childhood friend stands before me and speaks, "Don't ever forget me, my friend!" How can I? I used to paint landscapes in the beginning. Now I paint treescapes instead of landscapes.

I look at the trees of our world standing and serving mankind and other animals. They not only serve as the life-line of the living world supplying oxygen and fruits to us, but also give fillip to the thought process of the human mind. Buddha received his enlightenment under a Bodhi tree and Rabindranath Tagore wrote his great poems of Geetanjali sitting under a tree at his Shantiniketan garden. The nature of trees is to teach us forbearance and tolerance, as they offer fruits and shelter to even those people whose axe destroys them without remorse.

Ancient Indians used motifs of leaves, flowers and fruits in creation of their art works. They also gave important status to the trees by carving images of tree-Gods and Goddesses for the purpose of worship. The artist in me has seen the life and beauty of trees again and again throughout my life. In my paintings of treescapes, I have tried to express my feelings and gratitude to the beautiful trees, seen in swift and sweeping changes of lights, colours and movements through different seasons. I have realised the principles of life, growth and selfless existence in the trees which were created as first life of this planet by the creator. Trees and plants support the second and third life of animals and human beings of this planet. What I mean by third life is the life of ascent of human beings to higher consciousness of life divine.

I think humankind unlike other animals has a fund of surplus emotional energy which seeks its outlet in the creation of art works. My inborn love for colour sensations and pleasure of handling art materials keeps me fully engrossed with my art activities. When I was invited by Indusvista Art Lounge, Mumbai, to show case my paintings in March 2008, I accepted the offer without a second thought. My theme for the exhibition was 'Homage to Mother Earth'. The modern generation is inclined to believe that man with his knowledge and scientific discoveries can conquer and rule this world and its natural forces. But we also know that life and its evolution on this planet is not an accidental phenomenon. It was preplanned by the cosmic order of creations for evolution of life on this planet to supra-conscious level and self-realisation. I think nature's gift of art to the artist is a means for development of his personality by identifying himself with the natural world and its order.

My forty paintings in oil, acrylic and water colour were intended to pay homage to Mother Earth for giving us the first life in the form of trees to serve, sacrifice and sustain the second and third life of animals and human beings. The exhibits were treescapes expressing my love of nature. The art lovers' response to the show was a matter of great satisfaction in my creative activities. 'Homage to Mother Earth' was my ninth solo exhibition after my retirement from Sir J.J. School of Art, as a Professor of History of Art.

My first solo exhibition of 29th November 1987 was sponsored by Chetana Art Gallery at Kala Ghoda, Mumbai. It was a major event of success in my art activities before my retirement from Sir J.J.. The media, including television, Times of India and other newspapers gave good coverage of that exhibition without my personal attempts or approach for advertisements.

In visual art the image of the artist needs to be built for his popularity in the art market. That is the reason why artists of this and earlier centuries painted their self portrait and approached the media for their success. Public memory is very short and needs to be revived continually. A good friend of mine and well known character actor in the movies once told me that in the world of present consumerism, the painting is not art but selling a painting is art! I have not yet realised the truth of his statement. I continue to do paintings because of my inner compulsions. Forms and colours speak to me while I paint and I accept and respect their language as that of my own. Sometimes I speak with my own paintings even after completion and do whatever is desired to create a rhythm for both – i.e. me and my paintings. This is a process of expanding aesthetic vision or enlightening my own self.

Aesthetic visions differ depending on man's ability of perceptions and his cultural philosophy. When I was a professor of History of Art, I was invited to attend, 'Confrontations of East and West', a programme arranged at NCPA Mumbai. Major artists of India and the artists of Western countries including Canada, and Russia participated. I still remember the horror-sculptures of the young Canadian artist. He bluntly said that professor Bendre's works were no works of art! The shocking statement was by itself so horrific (like his sculptures) that the audience was stunned for a moment. It was a matter of that artist's perception and culture. Professor Bendre showed his magnanimity by keeping silent. Bendre's colourful canvasses depicted peace and love for Nature.

The paintings showcased in my first exhibition of 1987 were personal revelations of my emotions and sentiments of the life I lived. They were a kind of mixture of experimental works with many concepts and different expressive characteristics.

I think I was very much influenced by the art subjects I was then teaching, namely, History of World Art and Aesthetics.

One of my visitors to this exhibition was an American gentleman and consulting engineer of Tata's. He was looking intensely at each and every painting and finally came to my table and introduced himself. I was really glad to receive him for he had spent more than half an hour looking at my paintings. He said "I am working here in India, and my salary is not very high. I liked your paintings because they are bright and full of life. I am not buying to resell them. I have a habit of relaxing by looking at my collection of paintings every night before going to bed and every morning before leaving the room. I need to change my paintings on the walls whenever I feel like doing so. Will you give me some concession in the price?"

I was so delighted by his frank talk that, much against the wish of my sponsor, I gave him a fifteen percent discount. He surprised me by choosing three paintings from my first show. I also felt that art has its own purpose and that purpose is to create strong bond of love amongst human beings of this world, without distortions of facts, forms and rhythms of life.

Indian aesthetics maintains that suggestion in art is its virtue and strength while distortion is the result of an artists' weakness. Sometimes an artist distorts his forms for a specific purpose which can be accepted. In Modern Art practice there is confusion about good and bad art. Distortions are encouraged by some modernists and preferred as a necessary part of great art of the present century. I think distortions in art are reflections of the disturbed conditions of the artist's mind. Consider the painting –Les Demoiselles d'Avignon by Pablo Picasso in 1907. It was painted during the time when Picasso was inflicted by a sex-disease during his visits to commercial sex workers. His disgust and hatred for those women were expressed by sharp cuttings and distortions of facial features of those women. His purpose was to show the ugliness and not the beauty of the body and face. This was a time when Europeans did not believe in their own cultural background because of war and its ugly effects. Violence cannot be accepted as a standard for any culture and art. Fine art of painting should contain finer nuances of colours and forms to suggest noble qualities of humankind. Distortions cannot set a standard for good art.

Emotional links to the world at large are very powerful in our childhood because all new things and happenings in life are full of excitement and surprises. I have a graphic memory of my first journey to Karwar, when I was only six years old. The 15 miles long coastal road to Karwar from Avarsa is of scenic beauty. This serpentine road runs through mountainous terrain of thick forest with picturesque landscapes. The curvaceous descent from the higher mountain plane to the zig zag sea shore down below is like entering a new world of seascapes. The sight of rocky seashore to the left side of the road where sea waves continually break to form white bubbles of foaming water is a most beautiful welcome entry to Karwar town. Here I completed my high school education.

On the first night in Karwar, I was facing the sea through the window of my first floor house. The distant lighthouse of Karwar was lighting up the window at regular intervals of time, when I slept with a feeling of great excitement and fulfillment.

In the early morning when I opened my sleepy eyes I saw the most beautiful full moon on the horizon of the sea with its reflection and closed my eyes delighted.

I must have slept for a few minutes before I opened my eyes once again. To my shock and surprise the moon was no longer in the sky and the entire sea was painted orange-yellow. I felt sad and angry because I thought the vast sea must have swallowed the moon! Later in the morning my mother consoled me with an explanation that the sun and moon appear in the morning and at night respectively and disappear because they go to the other side of the world. I was not fully satisfied with my mother's explanation. I started watching the sky now and then. I am now convinced that my mother's statement of sun and moon must have given a new twist to my thinking process of questioning the how and why of everything in this living world.

I completed my high school studies from Hindu High School, Karwar and passed my matriculation (S.S.C.) examination in the year 1949, with credits in all subjects i.e., First Class, with distinction. I also passed two drawing grade examinations during my early school life. I came to Bombay

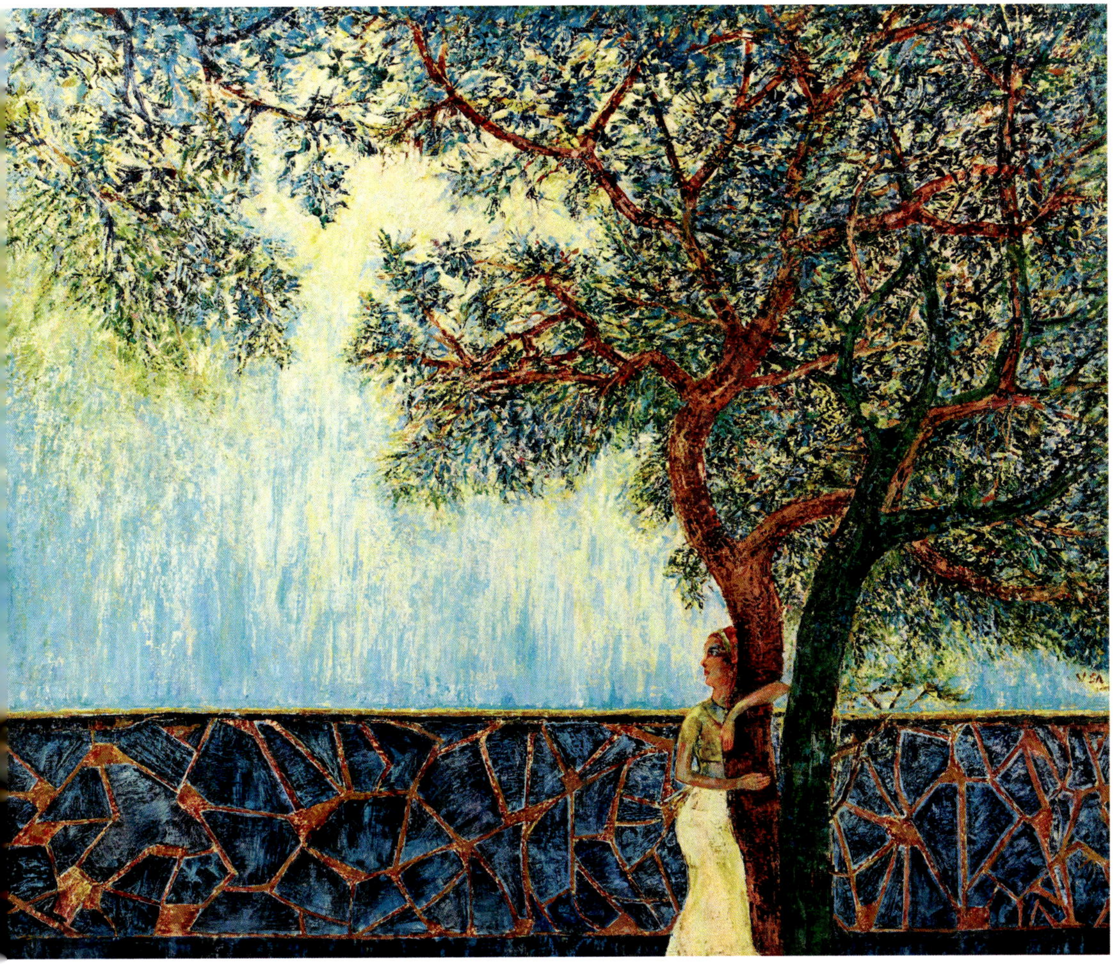

Two Together

48"x44" • Oil on Canvas

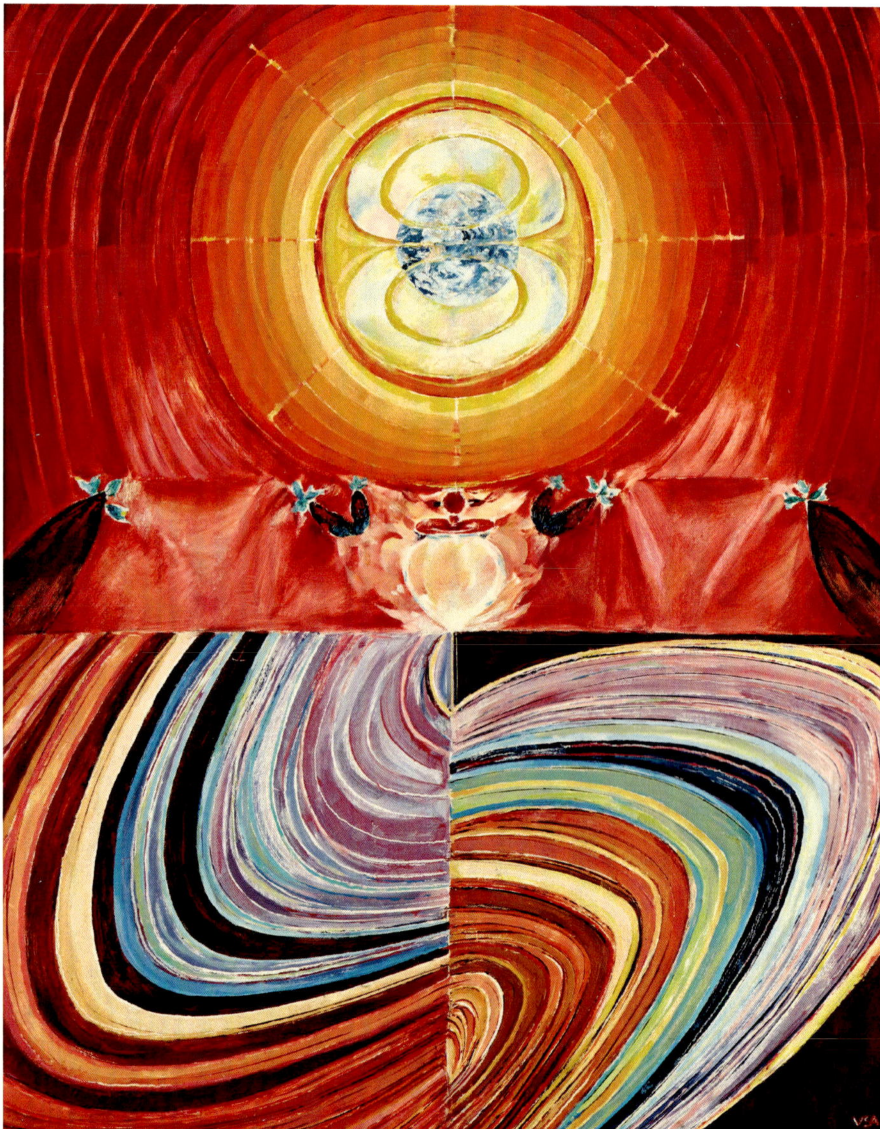

Homage to Mother Earth

24"x30" • Oil on Canvas

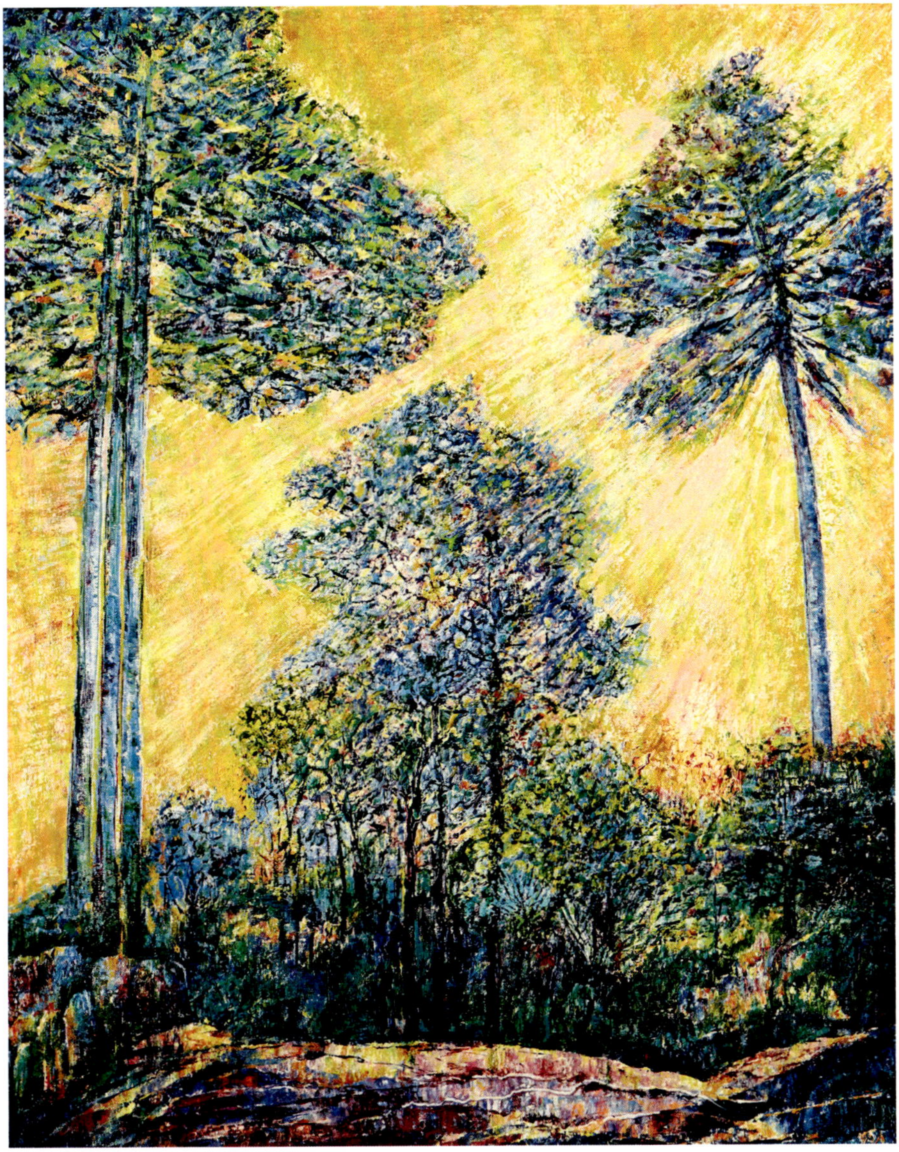

Treescape

24"x32" • Oil on Canvas

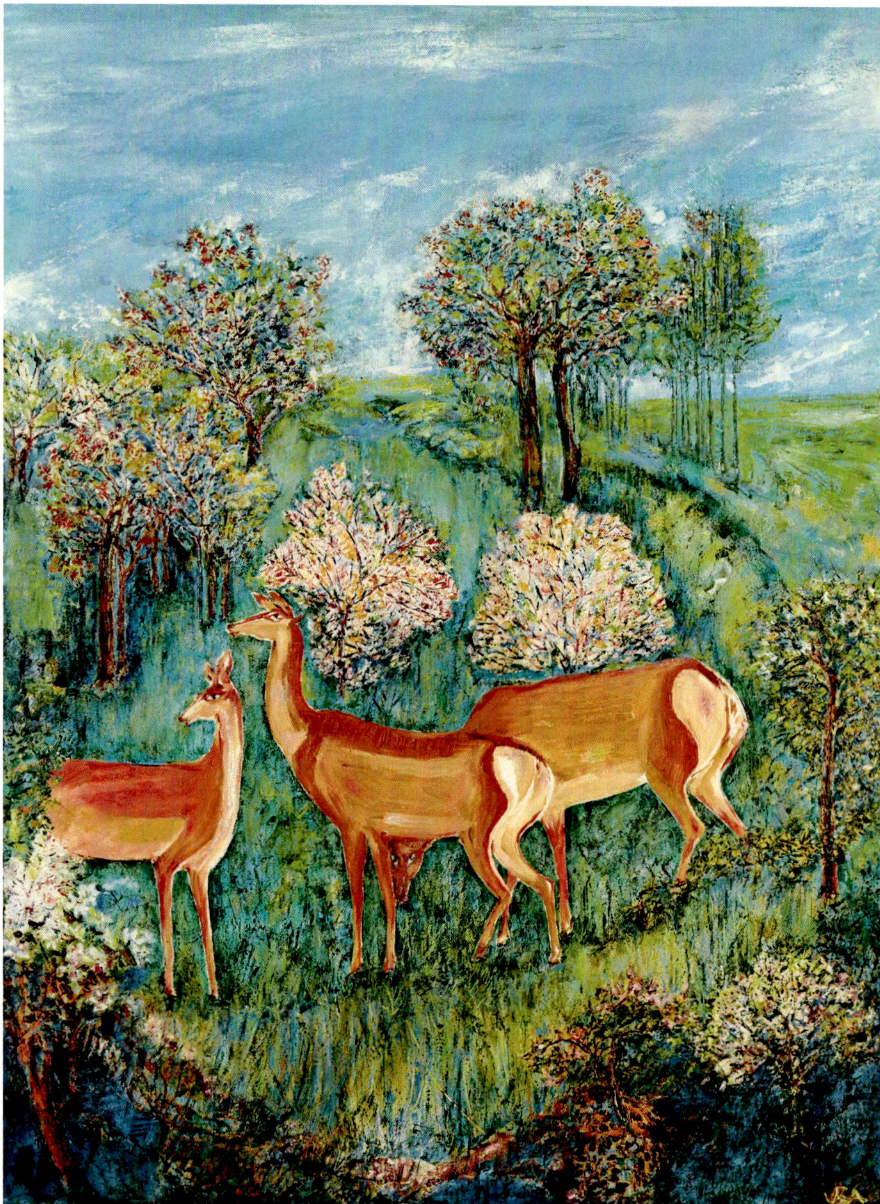

Deer Park

24"x32" • Oil on Canvas

for my further education in May 1949, and completed my degree course of B.A. with Philosophy and Psychology as special subjects. I joined Sir J.J. School of Art in the year 1952-53, as I was fond of drawing and painting. I completed both post graduation degree course of Bombay University, i.e. M.A. in Ancient Indian Culture with Art and Architecture and Govt. Diploma in Painting (G.D. Art).

Education and practice in fine art did not provide job opportunities during the first two decades of our independence and paintings were sold for a pittance in India. Many J.J. artists like F.N. Souza, Raza, Mohan Samant and others went to European countries for their livelihood. I joined the administrative service in Mantralaya but continued to paint for my personal pleasure. I then knew that art is the inner necessity of my mind and body.

I believe every individual is born with a destiny and his will power and actions determine the success of his achievements in this life. I was not happy with my administrative service in Mantralaya. One day I received an unexpected phone call from Professor V.N. Adarkar, the Director of Art, Maharashtra, asking me whether I was willing to join as a lecturer in the Sir J.J. Institute of Applied Art. He said he was planning to revise the diploma courses in art and he required a person of my qualifications. It was a God sent opportunity for me and I accepted his offer with gratitude.

The syllabus of teaching courses of both Fine Art and Applied Art were to be revised for the first time after the Indian Independence. Professor V.R. Amberkar, Madhav Satavlekar and I were entrusted with drafting the new syllabus. Subjects like History of Art and Aesthetics, which were not included in the old syllabus were made compulsory for the G. D. Art courses from the year 1969-70 onwards. After ten years, Sir J.J. School of Fine Art and the Institute of Applied Art were affiliated to the Bombay University. As a professor of History of Art, I was responsible for acquisition of slides and books from time to time, along with other visual aids for development of the History of Art department. The syllabus of graduation courses of the university comprised of History of World Art from prehistoric period to modern period. It included constructive criticism and appreciation of different styles and forms of arts. Before I retired in 1989, I was selected as a professor for the post graduate degree course of Sir J.J. Kala Mahavidyalaya.

It was a lucky coincidence that at the end of the academic year of my retirement in 1989, Sir J.J. teachers of all departments came together to hold an exhibition of their works in the J.J. campus. A catalogue of outstanding merit titled 'TEACHERS' was designed and circulated to the art lovers and critics. I cannot forget the initiative and talents of the Sir J.J. School of Art faculty members and students of that period who took part to make the event a grand success. Luckily for me, all my three paintings from that exhibition were purchased by Shri. Guha, then premises engineer of the Reserve Bank of India. I am happy that my paintings are displayed in the lounges of the Reserve Bank and NABARD.

After retirement from my academic obligations, I was free to engage myself solely in the creative work of my craving for the rest of my life. I even refused to accept requests and invitations for visiting professorship. I travelled from state to state in India to visit famous temples, historic places and palaces, museums and galleries to refresh my mind and vision of India. My exhibition of paintings in Jehangir Art Gallery in 1991 was a kind of mirror to the beauty of evergreen Kerala and was acclaimed by the art lovers of Mumbai. My next exhibition at Taj Art Gallery in March 1993 was also a great success and a matter of satisfaction of my retired life. Thereafter I had two solo exhibitions at Jehangir Art Gallery which were visited by enthusiastic appreciators and art collectors.

All India Fine Arts and Crafts Society, New Delhi, invited me to take part in their exhibition of senior artists of India and I was honoured by the President at a special function on 23rd February 1996 with a silver plaque and declared a veteran creative artist of India. I was also requested to take part in the 10 day art workshop conducted by the Art Society in Andheri, Mumbai, with 10 Delhi artists and an equal number from Mumbai.

Three canvas paintings of the size 3'x3' were presented by me at the end of our workshop to the F.A. & C. Society for the exhibition held at Yashwantrao Chavan Art Gallery, Mumbai. The paintings were sent to A.I.F.A. society, New Delhi, for exhibition by the society in New Delhi.

My art is the manifestation of the personal facts of my life. They are not the facts merely linked to my knowledge but linked to my emotional life and human sentiments. My paintings sing the song of nature and her elements, my attachments of innocent childhood and my relations with the world I loved. Intimate contacts with my teachers and other great people whom I admired with reverence nurtured the growth and progress of my personal life. My paintings are therefore personal facts of my life and defy analysis because they have immediate access to heart.

It is said that 'The style is the man'. But I am a man with many styles and techniques. An artist can produce a thousand different lines to express his emotional riches. A line for Bear can be different from the line for Beauty or Ball. In visual art, concepts and subjects can change the forms, styles and techniques in the process of creative activities.

Some art historians and art critics believe that the artist's intentions are important in recognising the great works of Modern Art. This statement had some significance in the context of the 20th century modern Western art when many new art styles or 'isms' were brought up with written manifestos by various groups of artists, philosophers and poets, supporting their work style in art. This revolutionary movement against the established values of many centuries of Western art has given freedom of practice to the global artists of the 21st century. The advantages of the universal language in the visual arts at any one period are obvious. I think a critical review of works of major artists of the world can expand the inner visions of the practicing artists of this century. The principal object of art is the expression of personality and not the production of beauty, whereas, the beauty in art has been the mere instrument and not its ultimate significance. The language of visual art is of forms, shapes and colours and that of music is sound. When we are looking at a painting or listening to music we are at once with the art personalities which are not abstract or analytical. The percipients should relax and enjoy the works of art. The truth and vital point in art cannot be discovered by analytical treatment, for the true principle of art is the principle of unity.

After I retired from teaching, I have painted more than two hundred paintings in oils, acrylics and water colours, and also exhibited them in more than ten solo exhibitions in the city of Mumbai. My early paintings were representative in kind, meaning mountain ranges with changing lights and shades of days and nights, seascapes in moonlight with fishing boats, landscapes in different perspectives, waterfalls and flowering trees suggesting different seasons of the year. I have painted more than fifty treescapes to indicate not only the beauty of swaying rhythms of trees but to suggest their importance to this living planet of evolutionary life. My portrait paintings of Rabindranath Tagore, Swami Vivekanand, Chatrapati Shivaji Maharaj and my twelve year old daughter and her pet dog are very personal to me and have not been exhibited so far. I have classified the above works as representative art because they can be easily recognised and identified with my emotional background of childhood. Also the forms in the paintings correlate with the natural world. Depending upon the art materials and medium used in the creation of these paintings my style and techniques have changed. Water colours on paper, acrylics and oil colours on canvas need different techniques and handling of mediums to satisfy the artist's object and design. Representative paintings need no titles for their recognitions.

Modernists define art as psychology and not anatomy. That means all art has its origin in psyche or mind, the mirror images of the seeming things of the world; meaning a photographic image is not considered as art. A photographer recognises the merit and magic of the object of the world with his aesthetic sense and clicks to get a fine photograph. But a creative painter perceives the objects with a creative eye and through a mental process of various adjustments, corrections and improvisations to the satisfaction of his aesthetic personality, transforms the very image into a symbol of his choice. Thus his art is abstract and personal and not a reflection of nature. His images assume the characteristics of his personality which is his art. The artists' concepts, imagination and techniques matter for his success. A masterpiece suggests the power and vital points of the art, which cannot be analysed by words. Thus, generally speaking, all fine arts are abstract by nature.

The question then arises; what is the significance of the terms 'Abstract Art and also Abstract Expressionism in Modern Art?' We know from the history of 20th century Western art about the Cubist movement of breaking nature's forms and structures into geometrical forms to rearrange them to create new compositions in visual art. This breaking up of smoothly continuous volumes into separate interlocking planes leads away from realism to a new concept of design independent of nature and its forms. This process involves analysis and synthesis of natural forms, without regards to their functions and structures in design. The images look as if disintegrating into their planes but there is something new about them. Against the background of the World Wars and disillusionment in their culture, Europeans wanted something revolutionary in the existing practice of art and creativity. Picasso and Braque had laid the basis for this new kind of painting which replaced the old pictorial space with a new kind of pictorial design. Cubist paintings with simplified forms and a shifting point of view presented an object as if seen from several different angles. In the ancient period, geometrical forms were considered pure forms and were used for decorative and spiritual purposes in art. Artist Kandinsky's colour experiments and their spiritual values were also made known to the art world. Modern artists like Mondrian, Naum Gabo, Pevsner and others created new designs with new materials for modern architecture. Sculptors who were influenced by the Cubist style created experimental human and animal forms with new concepts of their own. Thus the term Abstract Art is being used for that experimental art where the symbolic images in the compositions are imaginatively conceived by the artists without reference to Nature or its objects. The principle of abstract in art is, therefore, unity and vitality of human personality – both rational and irrational.

My Brush with Abstract Expressionism

We all know that the process of creativity involves both mind and body and that great abstract thoughts and truths are revealed by great minds. Wise men believe that sound mind is sound body. American artist Jackson Pollock's dancing, splashing and splattering colours on canvases directly from colour cans without a conceived design or composition brought a surprise shock to the contemplative art practices and styles of 20th century Abstract Art.

In early 20th century, German art style of figurative compositions expressive of extreme sufferings and distortions of mankind due to war and its disastrous effects on mind and body was named as Expressionism in art. Pollock's non-figurative art works produced under extreme conditions of mind and body under the influence of alcohol and music was renamed by critics as Abstract Expressionism, for, in his paintings there were no definite forms or figures. Logically speaking, Pollock's art style should have been named as 'Abstract Extremism' for it mixes paint, dance and music in a rare combination. It also encourages younger generations of artists to practice art with possible gimmicks. As a result, in India, traditional art and teaching of higher art courses were undermined by so called experts and critics influenced by Modern Art. They proclaimed winding and unwinding theories of art education and practice, thinking that art is only a fashion which must change with the time.

My abstract paintings are coloured by my own philosophy and concepts in art. I am convinced that visual art i.e. paintings and sculptures, are creations of talented artists because of their compelling inner necessity for expressions of feelings of love, joy and devotion for all things of the world, seen and unseen.

I believe inspiration, power and vitality of my paintings come from my imagination and emotional fire for realisation of my own concepts.

My concepts for abstract paintings are developed experimentally on the foundations of my knowledge and experiences of the natural and manmade world. My aesthetic sense and sensibility help me to experience the joy of creative actions and also guide my progress of the work till its completion.

My inborn skills give me the required confidence in handling the art material I love, and enable me to change the styles and techniques of my abstract paintings whenever I choose to do so. Imaginative contemplation is the source of all Abstract Art and it is also a method to reach a higher stage of consciousness in life. My art is linked to my spiritual personality which has loved and respected the good of all religions and the best of humanity. My spirituality is in the impulses and rhythms of my consciousness, which in turn, is the unity of world consciousness and its display. I think fine art is the technology of spiritual culture and consciousness, whereas, applied art is the technology for industrial culture and science of the world for development.

In my paintings, I use pure colours and superimpose them when required so that colours can vibrate with their natural intensity. I also adjust one area of colour to its neighbouring areas of colours and planes to achieve an overall unity of colours and their forms. In abstract paintings, I change my style and technique.

My intention is to create paintings corresponding to the order of nature because I am a part and parcel of nature. The influences of 20th century Modern Art were sometimes superficial as in the case of Cubism, based on a misunderstanding of certain characteristics of French artist Cezanne's works. My paintings are my means to enter into the nature's mystery of life and its unity on this planet.

Geometrical forms, considered to be pure and basic forms of visual art, can be used mainly for architectural, decorative and ornamental functions to serve art. They are also used for rituals and mystical functions of certain religious practices. I use them for colour-constructs in my abstract paintings. My abstract paintings include both geometrical and other symbolic forms of visual language to serve the purpose and expression of my concepts. My concepts are related to the acceptable universal truth discovered by science and religions of the world. Abstract subjects of my paintings are, for example – (I) $E=MC^2$, (II) Confluence, (III) Vibrations and Creation, (IV) Subconsciousness, (V) Surge of Consciousness, (VI) Homage to Mother Earth, (VII) Little Green is Left (VIII) Aranyika or Tree Goddess (IX) Sky and the Sea, (X) Sky and the City, etc.

Higher Art – A Discipline of Practical Training

Normally artists do not comment or write about their own creations. It may be because they do not have equivalent or appropriate words to explain their visual expressions in the verbal language. It is also possible that some of them think that there can be no alternate language to reveal the emotional surge of feelings generated and experienced by them in their visual creations. Majority of painters know that a good painting is unique by itself, if it is an expression of higher visual perceptions of an enlightened mind. I have always maintained that the pursuit and practice of fine art is a discipline to kindle life.

In my early childhood I was often attracted and excited by the visual world and her phenomenal changes of seasons and colours, and the shimmering lights of sunrise and sunset. Drawing and painting the beautiful environments, sites and objects were my passion which gratified my emotional urges. When I joined to study fine arts at Sir J.J. School of Art in 1952, I realised it was a discipline to reach my destination in this life. The renowned school, with its glorious past, and many disciplines of visual arts including painting, sculpture, metal-craft, ceramics, textile design and graphic print-making, was a temple of learning, surrounded by a beautiful garden for inspiration.

In the first year, the learning process of drawing and painting in art starts with drawing and sketching with pencils. It is said that a point goes for a walk to make a line. In nature, we have only shapes and solid forms, but no lines. Only human beings can draw lines with drawing pencils or pens. Artists can produce varieties of lines and forms to express their feelings with their drawings. A pencil point comes to life and moves with the sensitive fingers of an artist to make lines and forms of different shades and shapes. Symbolic and life like images emerge in response to conscious and subconscious directions from the artistic mind. This is the first phase of a discipline to control and learn the use of a simple medium of art, the pencil.

During the colonial rule in India, the syllabi for higher art at the School of Art were prescribed on the basis of the British School of Art in London. The British did not consider it worthwhile to bring the revolutionary tendencies of Western Modern Art to India. Instead, they thought it desirable to explore traditional Indian arts. Ajanta cave paintings were discovered and carefully studied by making their copies for exhibition in London. Subjects like History of Art and Aesthetics were not introduced for study in the School of Art till the year 1968. A discipline of intense practice and experience was emphasised in learning visual arts. Students were awarded a government diploma after five-year courses of painting and sculpture. They were equipped and prepared to face any challenges in the creative field of visual art.

But there were no buyers and art markets in India to help make it one's profession. However, some adventurous art graduates left India to settle in Western countries for making their art fuel a successful profession.

I believed, and still believe, that the practice of higher art is a means and end by itself for advancing human personality. I therefore decided to study in-depth various aspects of arts and cultures of ancient civilisations of the world.

I completed my post-graduation course of philosophy, psychology and ancient world civilisations and finally accepted the post of lecturer in the school of art in the year 1967.

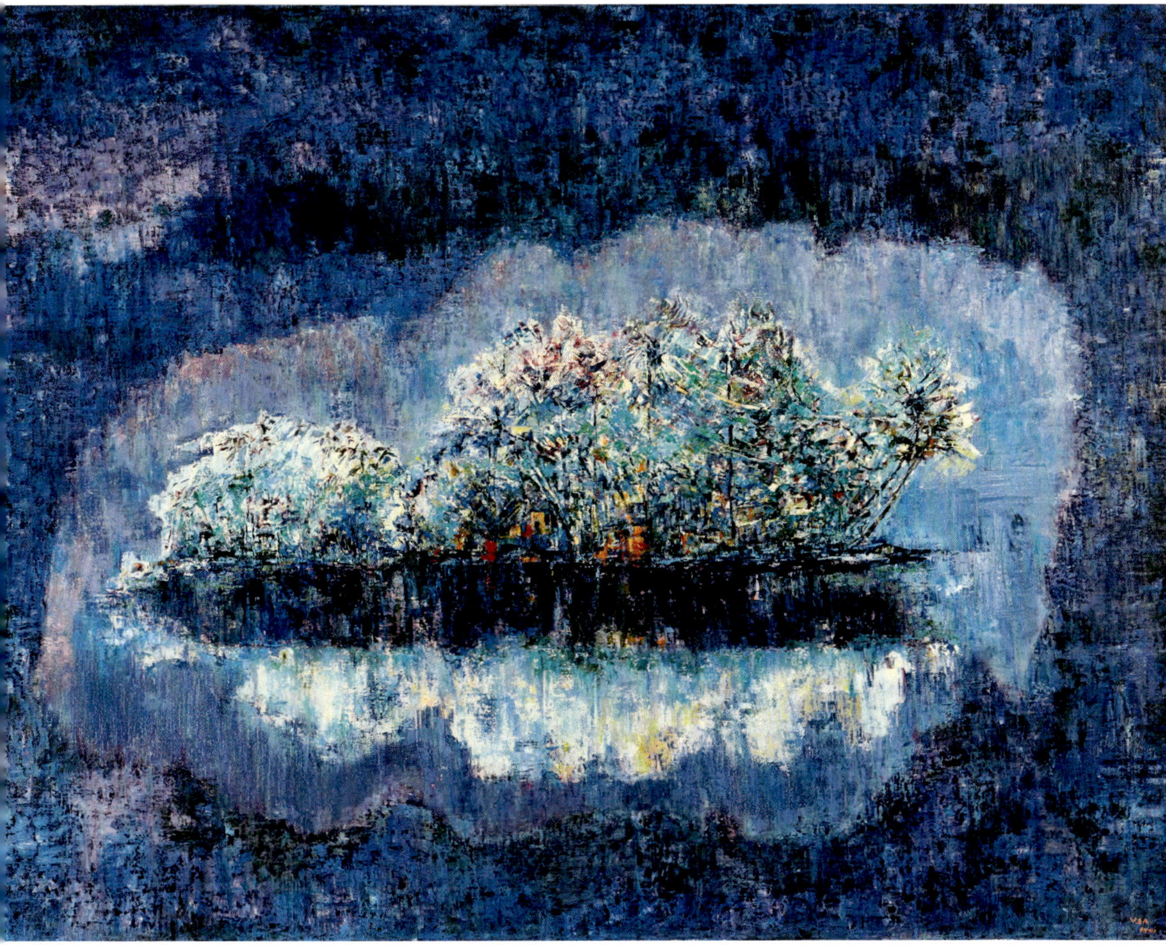

Life in Lagoons (Kerala)

40”x36” • Oil on Canvas

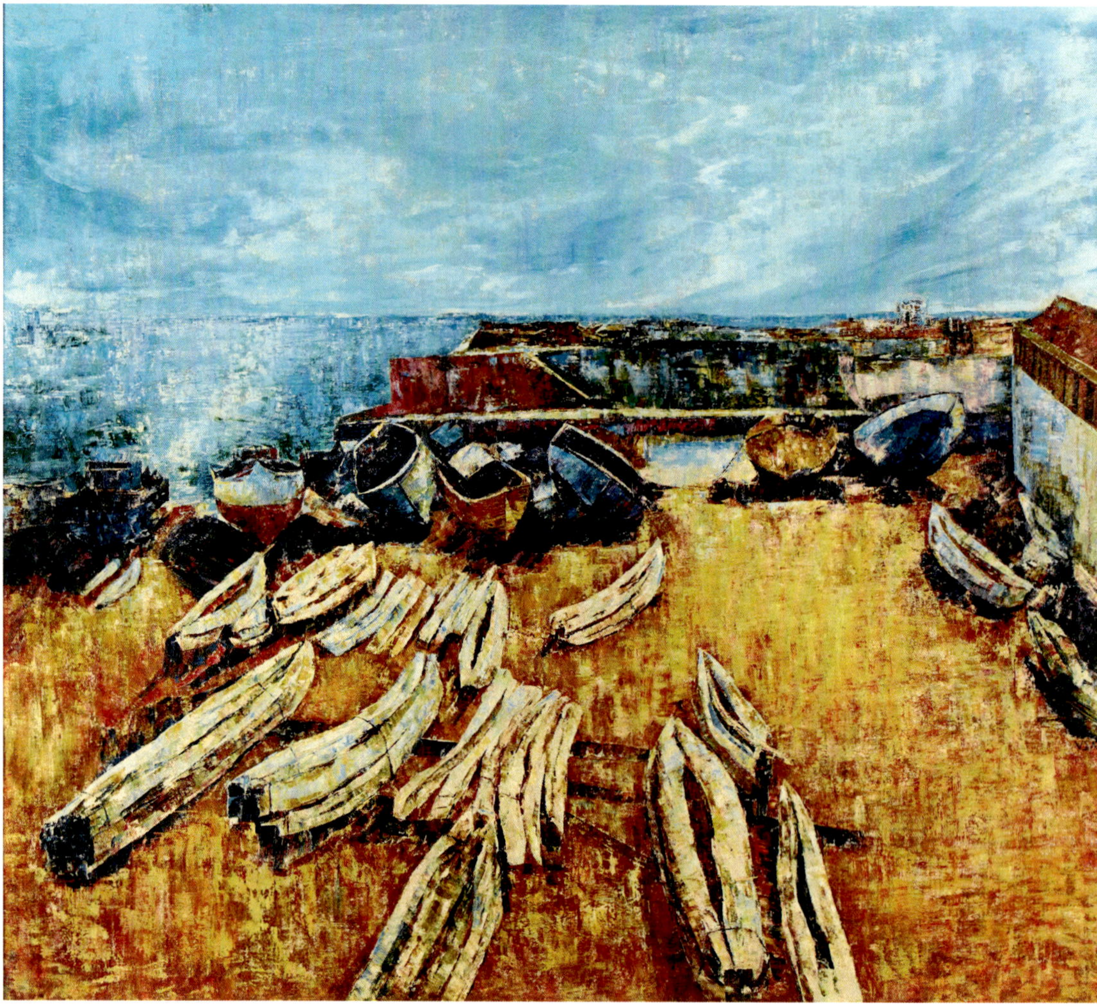

Fishing Boats (Kanyakumari)

46”x40” • Oil on Canvas

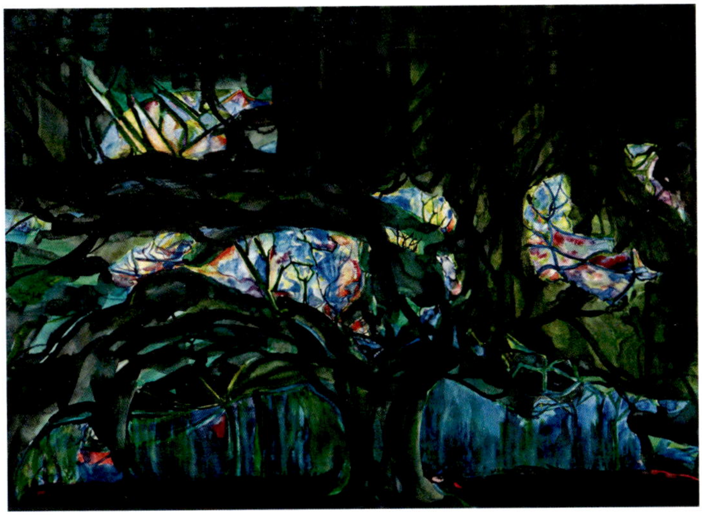

Treescape

26”x22” • Water Colour on Paper

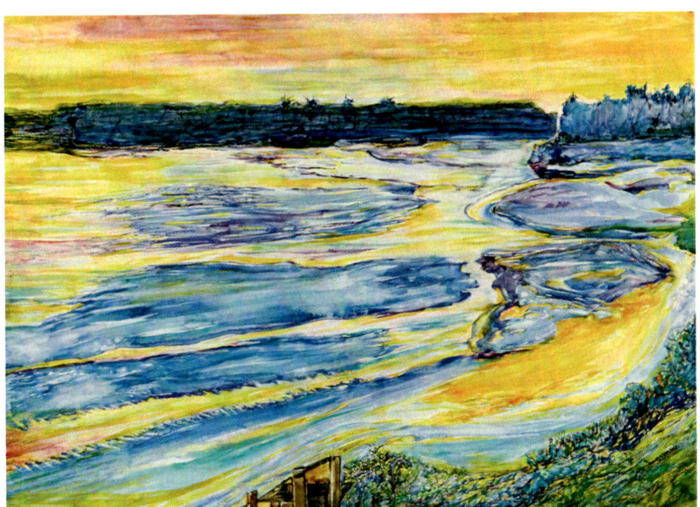

Confluence

26”x22” • Water Colour on Paper

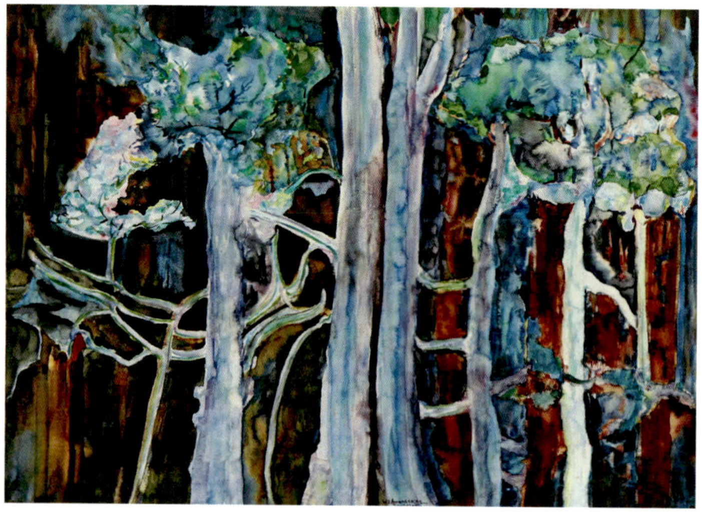

Treescape

26"x22" • Water Colour on Paper

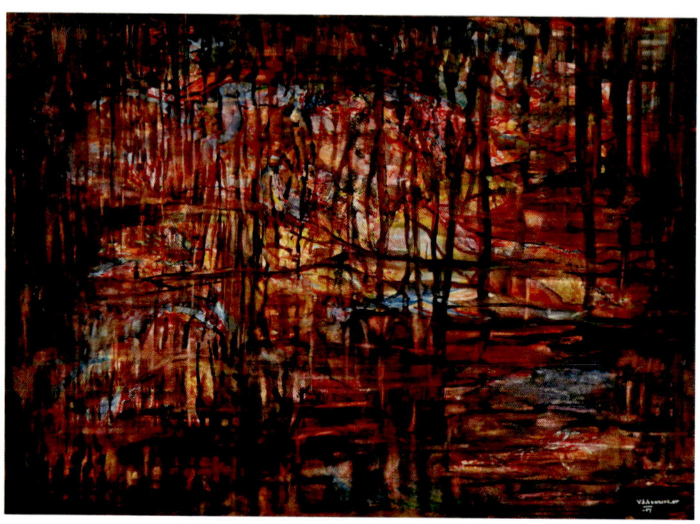

After the Cylone

26"x22" • Water Colour on Paper

A student of fine art enters into the world of colours only after perfecting his drawing and shading with pencils and charcoal-sticks. His pencil studies from both representative and memory drawings develop his sense of proportions of the objects of the world including animal and human figures. This practice builds an emotional tie of love and attachment for the world in which he lives. Distortions of images through lines and proportions were considered as human weakness, and negative feelings of disgust and hatred. I cannot think of reasons for distortion and its glorification in contemporary Modern Art. I never resorted to the practice of distortions in my work.

The practice and use of water colours in painting still-life and landscapes in the first year class at the school of art, was not new to me. Handling of water colours is a great excitement and pleasure to almost all art students. Water colours refer to water soluble colours. If you do not like your first choice of a particular colour you can immediately wash it off with a clean brush and water. Once you know its quality of transparency, you can start using thick and dilute colour to create an impression of floating colour forms on the paper. Beauty of water colour is seen in its transparency. One does not mix white colour in it to get a particular tone. White paper serves that purpose. Imagination, skill and speed are required to blend the colours on the paper before the colours dry up. Water colour and its practice in art, helps the art students to acquire colour sensitivity and its intuitive use in painting with speed, because, colour tones are created on the paper itself without a colour palette.

Unlike water colours, oil colours last for hundreds of years without fading. Oil colours are mixed on the palette to prepare required tones and shades before using them with a brush or painting knife. Colours are applied on the canvas by super imposition and the technique is known as impasto. Colours are also applied in juxtaposition to create colour vibrations or resonances. Before mixing oil colours, it is necessary to know a bit about colour and its chemistry to avoid fading of colours in the near future.

Acrylic colours and pastels on the other hand are quick in drying and comfortable in handling.

In my opinion, all colours are beautiful with their quality to shine and arouse an emotion. But an artist's conscious and subconscious choice of colours and its application matter in his creative paintings. The process in visual art starts with the artist's personal experiences and ends with a sense of satisfaction and relief to the artist. A colour sensitive artist can see the different, pure colours coming forward or receding, depending on their natural quality to shine, when applied on a white surface. Prepared tone and shades of different colours can also be used to achieve a play of colours and their movements in visual compositions. Pure colours and colour tones have distinct natural brightness to create their own independent forms and shapes when applied side by side on white surfaces of paper or canvas, as colour constructs in paintings.

A significant Russian painter of The Blue Rider group of Modern Art, Vasily Kandinsky, carried his research into the emotional and psychological properties of colours, line and shape. He made his statement with his two kinds of paintings:

(a) Compositions: Work of art with use of line, shapes and colours with conscious planning and selection of colours.

(b) Improvisations: Work of art without planning but only with subconscious selection of colours.

He declared the works with no resemblance to the objects of the world as

(a) Abstract Art, and (b) Spiritual Art.

His logic of spirituality in art has failed to inspire me and my spiritual awakening. But it has inspired American artist Jackson Pollock to throw colours on canvas and paint with a dancing performance.

Kandinsky's theory and practicals on spiritual art by selection and application of colours only through the subconscious state of mind is not feasible and correct. When an artist is free to concentrate and contemplate in his waking condition, his whole consciousness, inclusive of subconsciousness, is involved in his creative activity. If he works under hypnotic trance when he is no longer fully conscious, his expressions are not spiritual. Dream images of the subconscious mind in sleep, are no longer considered spiritual in art and life. Spiritual visions are possible only when a person reaches a state of supra-conscious mind through meditation and is totally absorbed in the object of his meditation.

Spirituality of colours, if any, can be realised in paintings when a colour sensitive artist explores the refractive powers of colours and their beauty in nature's elements. Colours come with light and go with light. In reality, they are part and whole of white sunlight. Magic of colours is perceived in the sky and the sea, on the mountains and treetops, as the morning sunlight glitters and sparkles through the plants and flowers of the earth to reveal the beauty of colours.

Spiritual sensation and freshness of colours can be experienced in the series of (oil colours on canvas) paintings by Laxman Shreshtha. His Abstracts, influenced by the Himalayan range of mountains, emanate both colour and light from within the devotional and creative art of India.

Paintings - The Experience of the Eye

Contemporary secular artists of the modern world have accepted philosophy, psychology and aesthetics as basis of their abstract paintings and sculptures. Philosophy means love for knowledge. (Philos=Love, Sophia=Knowledge, in Greek). When a great Greek philosopher was questioned what he had discovered after his continual reading of books, he promptly replied, "more I read more I discovered how ignorant I am".

It is a fact that book-knowledge remains in the books only. True knowledge comes to us at once with experience when the mind is enlightened. Put a pinch of sugar on the tip of your tongue and you know what sugar is, instead of reading descriptions of it in so many words. Paintings and sculptures are objects of experience of the eye of the artists and artistic minds. The intuitive eye of an artist is at its best when the creativity is in progress, and, it brings in the higher and finer qualities in the process itself.

The aesthetic sense of the artist helps him to maintain proportion, balance and rhythm in the forms, and their arrangements in paintings and sculptures. Selection of particular colours and their relative use of shades and tones, with the artist's brush strokes, make a painting unique and beautiful. Creation of experimental abstract painting helps the artist to innovate new forms and techniques which stimulates his sense of abstract beauty in visuals.

Psychology is the science of human psyche or mind. The nature of 'Mind' itself is the abstract reality.

Right from the ancient Vedic period Indian psychology explored the depth of human mind through yoga practices. Yoga controls the thought-waves in the mind. Mind (chitta) is a faculty within us which records the sense impressions of the outside world, and, classifies those impressions with its discriminative intelligence and reacts to them. The ego-sense of the mind stores such impressions as individual knowledge.

The individual behaviour of a human being is subject to his inborn faculties, environments, education and ambitions in life. The mind controls the human activities. The power and the quality of the human mind is subject to three 'gunas' or attributes of the body-mind. They are 'tamasic' i.e. dark, 'sattwik' white, and 'rajasic'. The active third force 'Rajas' helps to maintain the balance and equilibrium of the individual's characteristics. Will power of the mind helps to control the individual's activities with discriminative personal intelligence.

Indian psychology also indentifies seven centres of consciousness along the central nerves of the spinal column where the mind dwells. The resting position of the mind on any one of the six ascending conscious centres decides the nature and power of the human mind. If the mind dwells at the heart in the forth centre, the man experiences spiritual awakening. The control of mind and its powers by regular practice of yoga has proved this point beyond doubt.

Sigmund Freud's investigations are only the early stages of modern psychological enquiry and, therefore, his conclusions cannot be accepted as final. He has himself described his works as only the beginning of a pathway into the unconscious for an important advance in our knowledge.

Higher art practice is also concerned with spiritual and metaphysical aspects of art. Raja Yoga indicates that the mind-body has only one life-force. This force expresses itself in different ways at different levels of consciousness. It may impel a man to paint a picture, say his prayers, run a race, or have sexual intercourse. But it is always the same force, and is the potential energy which can be used for higher or spiritual purpose to kindle life. It is the level of higher consciousness of mind and not the subconscious mind which brings in the spiritual in art.

Sexual images are created by those painters and sculptors whose conscious level rests below the navel regions of the spinal nerve centre. Such images are not carved or painted inside an Indian temple. Iconic images with their symbolic significance are spiritually inspiring and they are always inside the temple and churches. They are the visions of devout artists and saints, who are enlightened by higher levels of consciousness of mind. There is nothing spiritual in Tantra paintings of India, or Kendinsky's improvisation theory of art.

All sincere artists aim for perfection in their works. Perfection of the body includes beauty, grace and strength. The perfection of the mind includes progressive concentration, contemplation and meditation on objects and forms, by using sense-organs outside the confines of the body. My art is both abstract and real at the same time, because I have always tried to express the unity in diversity of forms and colours in nature. The truth of existence is that the forms and expressions of an object may change, but all these changes of form and expression have existed and will continue to exist potentially within the object itself in an un-manifested, subtle form. Power of a painting with its characteristic expression contributes to the merit and quality of a painting. Spiritual and metaphysical elements in paintings and sculptures are the expressions of heightened consciousness of the meditative artist. Such expressions of forms and colours with powerful and subtle contents, create an atmosphere of ecstatic joy and excitement when the percipient is in communion with its contents. The medium of painting and sculpture as a discipline of higher art can be used to reach the most sublime realms of spiritual expansion. The artist can come close to the spiritual rhythm of the cosmos through his art by establishing communion with the inner reality.

Focus on My Painting

The most fascinating thing about painting is its unpredictable element which comes from eliminating all restraints in creative activity. Thus even my landscapes in their ultimate analysis become a play of energetic forms in space seeking new relationships and revealing an abstract reality of my own personality.

My experimental attitude to seek this new reality is the outcome of reinterpretation of art forms and aesthetic theories which has been my major concern for past several years. Thus through the process of painting I seek to probe into a new aesthetic vision, and at times make a simple statement in colours and forms. This experimental process is self-purifying and revealing.

In this continually changing world my style and technique have changed but my aim and purpose have remained constant, i.e. to see and seek the dynamism of cosmic life that pulsates throughout the world of objects with the magical beauty of metaphysical and mystical being.

Many a time the artist's intentions are deciding factors for the value judgment of his paintings. This is because the Abstract Modern Art often confuses the beholder for want of proper insight. I, therefore, consider it useful to explain my own concepts in some of my paintings reproduced in this book.

My interest in Indian philosophy i.e. 'Vedaant' and the theory of evolution of life, as well as the scientific discoveries of abstract forces in our universe, inspired me to seek the reality of our existence through the medium of creative paintings.

Dynamic forces in vibration produce elements of life everywhere on this planet. This concept inspired me to paint my first abstract painting titled 'Elements of Creations'. This painting depicts moving rhythmic lines coming together from various points in the space with a vibrative force, and meet to defuse and create subtle and fresh elemental forms like leaves and flowers. In the intervening space of rhythmic lines, new but incomplete forms of colours can be recognised imaginatively. i.e. the beginnings of new life in creations.

Some contemporary artists create a series of paintings with just one concept and style. I prefer to give importance to new concepts and techniques. I have always painted with changing concepts, styles and techniques. My concepts change with my objects and paintings. The very process of painting enriches my experience and knowledge for bringing in perfection in my works.

After abstract compositions of line and their rhythms, I have tried in some paintings to establish rhythms of circular forms and their movements in space. My subsequent paintings were only with geometrical forms, which are known as basic or pure forms in fine art. Squares, rectangles, and triangles in almost pure colours were arranged and rearranged in order to experience balance and equilibrium of moving structural forms and shapes. In the process, the structures were broken to suggest new relationships in movements. Creations and destruction of structures and forms suggested a metaphysical aspect in those paintings. One could see the happening and not happening i.e. birth and destruction side by side. Some of my other old paintings titled 'Colour Constructs' and 'The Temple without Idol' are the creations of continuation of this concept. My later paintings of 2009 titled 'Subconsciousness' and 'Surge of Consciousness' are representations of change of concepts in Abstract Art.

The artist's love for nature and its scenic beauty in different seasons is expressed in landscapes, treescapes and seascapes, in changing lights of the morning and evening. My paintings (in water colours, acrylics and oil colours) of mountain ranges, waterfalls, river banks and forests covered with varieties of trees with colours and flowers are still in my collection. Thickets and paths in the forests were for some time the focus of my attention. I have taken much delight in painting them.

My canvas painting (4'x5') titled, 'Aranyika' i.e. tree-goddess is a candid example of my love and respect for trees. Trees have served this planet and the evolution of life on it, by standing and waiting, as the first life of service to the animal world. Without trees animal life cannot sustain by itself. Trees give generously without expectations. My tree-goddess is the anthropomorphic image of existing power providing selfless service to mankind.

My solo exhibition in March 2009, sponsored by Indusvista Art Lounge, Mumbai, I decided to pay homage to mother Earth. I painted more than 40 paintings of only treescapes for that exhibition. A symbolic representation of our planet in space, suspended by magnetic forces at its two poles, and a seated posture of a human at the bottom with a 'Kalash' of offerings in between, was specially painted and exhibited.

I have no botanical interest in trees like painter Paul Klee of Bauhaus school. My love for trees is aesthetical and ethical. Standing and swaying trees in different light and shades with their seasonal flowers and colours are the natures own creative principles of rhythms and beauty. My painting of each tree is intended to explore different aspects of evolution of first life on this planet. To my mind every tree is distinct with its forms, colours and content. They are individual personalities of my treescapes.

Mountains are beautiful to look at from a distance. They are nature's vast canvases showing a range of different colour hues spread between the sky and earth. But the experience of tracking mountainous regions is thrilling. My mountains are my experience of this thrill.

Some of my abstract paintings have a start without a concept. It is like a game of hide-and-seek of forms, colours and their light. I know painters cannot paint light and when there is light then only we can see colours. My attempts in some paintings are to paint the refractions of colours and their light. If the reality of diamonds is an illusion, my paintings are also an illusion like all plastic art. I have titled them 'My Diamonds'.

The world of 21st century is the world of science and technology that dominates modern life and living. It is interesting to note the findings of Vedantic philosophers (Rishis) and the modern scientist's confirmation that the Universe is comprised of only energy and mass or particles. The great scientist Albert Einstein had explained this truth in his mathematical formula $E=MC^2$ (E=Energy, M=Mass and C=Speed of Light). Monism explained in Vedanta distinguishes material world as transcendental i.e. ever changing Maya, meaning appearance. The reality is the one spiritual energy, meaning Brahma.

My painting titled, '$E=MC^2$ – Vedanta', is visualised with speed of ascending rays of colourful light which transforms the image of Lord Ganesh into bright light in the painting. This painting is an expression of abstract reality of both science and Indian religious philosophy. A concept always empowers the painting and its reality of the abstract truth.

--------------------x---------------------

This book includes the photo prints of some of the old and new paintings of the author in different mediums. Reproduction of paintings here is to illustrate the changing concepts and the resulting changes of styles and techniques.